SISTER

PASTOR

- Practical Guidelines for Minister's Wives -

CHEREE' HASTON

PUBLISHING

Atlanta, GA

First Edition

First Printing

Edited by Mark Haston

Cover design and photography by Julie Haston

Printed in the United State of America

To contact the author, please email:

bernice.wright@thetabonline.com

DEDICATION

With a grateful heart I would like to dedicate this book to my pastor, my editor, my husband, and my biggest supporter, Mark Haston.

Mark, you cannot imagine what your influence has meant to my life. I adore you.

And to my three beautiful daughters, Julie, Riley and Mackenzie, you are treasures to my life. Thank you for loving me unconditionally and keeping laughter and joy present in our home.

Thank you to the Sister Pastors in my life, especially my mother, Sherry, my mother in law, Aileen, and my grandmother, Martha.

Thank you to Pastor Michelle Steele of Faith Builders International. You are my friend.

I would also like to acknowledge the team of supporters, intercessors and staff who made this book possible. Without your efforts to encourage and at times push me in my quest to see this work published, I would still be staring at a half empty computer screen.

And to Priscilla Ezonnaebi, of Live1010 Life Coaching, I probably *could have* done this without you, but I probably *would not have*! Thank you for your investment into my life and ministry! You are a gift to the body of Christ!

CONTENTS

1.   Walking the Tightrope of Relationships

2.   Finding Your Place

3.   Dealing with Mean People

4.   Dealing with Stupid People...Bless their Hearts

5.   Dealing with Trauma

6.   The Sacrificial Lamb: It's up to you...well, sometimes

7.   The Diva Syndrome: We've been called to serve

8.   40 Rules to Live By Everyday

INTRODUCTION

Minister's wife. The title can conjure up a hundred thoughts in a matter of seconds, and the women who carry that title are as varied and different as the churches they serve. Maybe when you think of "minister's wife", you think of a sweet grandmother with soft skin, the church's best pot roast recipe, and someone who gently called you "honey." Possibly your mind goes back to a piano-playing, bun-hair having, alto-singing superwoman. You might even visualize a snotty, pretentious diva that not so secretly ran the church through her puppet named "Pastor." Or just maybe, hopefully, you visualize a well balanced woman of God that knew how to be both sweet and sassy. The non-church world has its vision of what a pastor or minister's wife should look like too. We are pulled in every direction and given opinion after opinion of who we should be, what we should look like, and how we should operate, not only on Sundays, but through the week as well. We live in a spotlight without the perks of "celebrity." The parsonage is the proverbial glass house. You might feel like it has become your own personal palace or maybe even your prison. Whatever your mental picture, I hope to share with you throughout this book some realistic and practical ways to positively influence the people you serve in the ministry!

If you're going to take the time to read this book, I will take the time to properly introduce myself. My name is Cheree'. I love Jesus, the ministry, and a great cup of coffee. With the exception of Christ, my family is the most important thing in the world to me. I have been married to my pastor, Mark, for 18 years. We have 3 daughters (Julie, Riley &

Mackenzie) and 2 female dogs. He is a blessed man. Mark and I have been in full time ministry our entire marriage. As a matter of fact, we moved our furniture into the youth pastor's parsonage one week before our wedding and began our tenure at that church the day we got back from our honeymoon. I am a third generation pastor's wife and I'm proud to be called such. That's a miracle in itself! Most of my closest friends are minister's wives and I pray that I am raising 3 ladies who will go into full time ministry. So, as you can imagine, this is a subject very dear to me. I must tell you, however, that although I love the ministry, the paths it's taken me down have not always been smooth ones. Some days I've felt as though I was being drug down these paths by a moving car! But when the dust settled and bandages were applied, I was at peace, a peace that came from knowing that I was in the center of God's purpose for my life.

My heart beats for ministers and their families. My prayer is that you will sense that as you turn these pages. Over the years, I've made more than my share of mistakes. I have watched my friends make them too. I want to help you avoid those same blunders so you can evade the heartaches they bring. I've also succeeded in some areas, as have many of my colleagues. I want your time invested in this book to result in a harvest of success and achievement to your life! If one small thing in this book makes a positive difference in your ministry or helps you avoid a potential pitfall, my investment in your life will be worth it! You can LOVE your life and the ministry to which you've been called! So sit back, grab a cup of coffee, and let's see which of my embarrassing blunders you can most identify with. Hey, if nothing else, you won't feel so bad about yourself!

CHAPTER 1

Walking the Tightrope of Relationships

When I was a little girl, I loved to watch the circus on television. My favorite act was the tightrope walker. I was amazed at the fluidity with which the men and women would not only walk, but sometimes hop and even dance along that tiny little rope. It wasn't until I went to a live circus that I realized the true height of the tightrope. I covered my eyes as she would glide effortlessly across the rope. My heart raced when I looked at how far she would fall if she ever lost her balance. I saw the net underneath her, but the distance still made me shudder. She seemed, however, perfectly calm. The only way she could master the tightrope was to master her balance. As an adult I realized, that's the life lesson: when you figure out balance, you can handle the narrowest paths. Relationships in the ministry must be handled with care. They can make or break you. They are not a juggling act, they are a balancing act. In this chapter, we'll explore how to balance the different relationships in your life so that you can glide across any narrow place you encounter.

Relationship #1 – Your Relationship with Christ

Your relationship with Christ is the number one, most important relationship in your life. As we'll discuss later, every type of relationship you have needs to be healthy, but if your relationship with Jesus isn't what it should be - nothing else matters. Without Him, what would you be doing in the ministry anyway? We've all been guilty of being so busy doing the work of the Lord, that we've neglected Him. I have made a determination in my life to spend time with Him every day. Because of all of the hats that I wear, I spend time with Him many different ways. Sometimes I sit quietly in the early morning hours while everyone is still asleep. Other times, I talk to Him while I'm doing my hair or ironing my clothes. I love to pray during my house cleaning days or sing to Him while driving in my car. Whatever the manner, I'm determined to get it done.

I've sat in the services where someone soberly testified how they get up at 4:00 am and spend two hours in prayer and two hours in Bible study. They say anything less is just pitiful and pathetic. I've left those meetings feeling like the rankest of sinners and promised God I'd meet Him in the kitchen at 3:30 AM, but it never happened - so the guilt ensued. I can't begin to express to you how vital it is that you make time for your relationships; most of all with Jesus. No matter you're schedule, you've just got to find a way. In the crazy world you live in, only you can figure out how. No matter how I try to cover it up, I know when I'm not spending quality time with the Lord and His Word. And you will know it, too. I can tell you this, if it's not on a daily basis, you're asking for trouble. As ministers, we must make time with the Master. His Word is to be our lamp and our light. It is bread to our souls and life to our bones! Without it, our spirit man will starve to death. As with any relationship, if you treat it passively, it will crumble. Imagine if you only spoke a few words to your spouse every couple of days, and even that was driven by guilt. How quickly would you find yourselves drifting apart? I have learned that my prayer time is not to be spent finding the most eloquent phrases to fall from my lips, it's to be spent communicating with my Father. I have wept to Him. I have been angry with

8

Him. I have laughed with Him. As long, as I commune with Him, He always draws me nearer. When I cry, He comforts me. When I am angry, He speaks peace. When I am joyful, He sings over me! There are times when I read His Word out loud to Him and His presence fills the room. The more time you spend with Him, the more He will teach you how to pray.

Who is God to you? The Word says, "the fear of the Lord is the beginning of wisdom" (Psalm 111:10). Well, I grew up with the fear of the Lord, alright. I was afraid of the Lord! It was a mindset I developed through years of seeing God's Word as a book of rules & regulations. I fully understand that the Bible is not a book of suggestions and by God's grace I now see the Word as my daily bread. My relationship with the Lord has evolved from being under the great God of judgment to truly knowing Abba Father. I am very frank (as you'll come to realize) about my own journey. I made the worst rookie mistakes, even after being far into my walk with God - but there I met His great mercy! It is very important that I know the God that I teach people about. I had to figure out who He was to me.

Here are Some Things God IS NOT

1. A Liar

Every word He speaks is true! Only Satan is described as "a liar and the father of it" (John 8:44). The Word actually says about God, "He is not a man that He should lie" (Numbers 23:19). It is the tactic of Satan to get us to doubt God's Word and His promises to us. If he can make you doubt the Word, you will ultimately doubt God and His love for you. Stop the enemy in his tracks! When thoughts of doubt enter your mind, remind yourself of Philippians 4:6-8. There Paul tells us to never worry about anything. Instead, we're to go before the Father with our situations. When we do, we'll find peace that passes all human understanding. Then it says to keep our minds focused on good, lovely, praise-worthy things. When you are tempted to doubt the goodness and truthfulness of God, set your mind on praising Him for healing, redemption, restoration, provision, kindness, peace, faithfulness, and on and on and on! He is true to His Word!

2. Sadistic

God is not a spiritual "Robin Hood" who takes from some of His children to give to others. For example, have you ever heard someone say at a funeral, "Oh, God must have needed another angel" or "He took your loved one so that someone else could learn a lesson?" These people may mean well, but that is not the God we serve! The Bible says He causes all circumstances to "work together for the good of His people" (Romans 8:28). He doesn't cause the circumstances. Why would God take my child just so that you could learn something? It's just not His nature. He doesn't love you more than He loves me and vice versa. However, living in a fallen world and dealing with circumstances we don't always understand, God steps in to be sure that good will come of it somehow, someway! We are told that it is "His pleasure to do good for His people when we seek Him" (Luke 12:31-32). His mercy and goodness endure from generation to generation!

3. Forgetful

I love the song that Israel Houghton wrote called "I am not Forgotten"! It's such an upbeat reminder that God doesn't

10

forget us or His promises to us. I've learned the hard way that it's not seed-time & harvest. It is Seed....Time....Harvest. When you are in the "time" phase, it can feel as if not only God, but the entire world has forgotten you. When seed is planted in your life, there must be time in order for the fruit to come into full maturity.

I have been pregnant for 27 months of my life! Whew! That's a long time. But here's the truth, if I had forced the babies to come I would have in essence aborted those pregnancies. And if the "ground" hadn't been right for the seed, the pregnancies would have miscarried. I spent the entirety of those months wishing every day to hold my babies. But I knew that they needed time to grow. I didn't sit around angry at God because I was as big as a house...well, most days I didn't. The point is that I knew I had to wait. As much as the desire was there to hold and touch and literally see what I'd been waiting for, I knew it was for the best. There were lots of days near the end of my pregnancies that I found 100 reasons why that day was the perfect day for the birth. But I made it through day after day until the time came. All three of our daughters were born healthy, happy and at the right time. God did what needed to be done in my body and in the bodies of my babies. Why then do I have difficulty accepting that God is still at work in the other seed of my life? You see, what I decided to do until the birth was to prepare for the arrival. What are you doing to prepare for the arrival of God's promises in your life? Just because I couldn't see my baby didn't mean I wasn't absolutely sure that I was having one. The closer I got to the birth, the more obvious the impending delivery was! I looked as if I would pop if the baby didn't come soon! How do you look in your spirit? Do you still fit into your "old clothes" or is this promise affecting every area of your life?

This patience not only works with the seed we plant (seeds of finance, prayer, fasting, time, etc.), but also with the seed that is planted inside of us. That seed is the Word of God. If there are scriptures you are declaring over your life (and I certainly hope there are), continue to cultivate that seed through faith and consistency. It WILL come to pass! Harvest time is on its way! You are not forgotten!

Here are Some Things God IS

1. Forgetful

Ok. I just confused some of you. I'm so sorry to my blonde sisters. Just kidding! Don't put the book down. Read on. The same God, who never forgets us, has made one of the most compassionate choices I've ever seen. He chooses to forgive and forget our sins. Honestly, take a moment and wrap your mind around that fact. There are some of you reading this book right now who are in some form or fashion experiencing guilt. You've made a mistake, asked for forgiveness, but you are still trying to make penance. Our loving Heavenly Father never asked you to do that. For far too long I operated this way. Every time something negative happened in my life, I somehow saw it as a result of my already repented sin or some thought of doubt even when I hadn't acted on it. Obviously, we understand that certain actions have certain results. For example, if you are involved in an extra-marital affair or fornication, you are putting yourself at risk of becoming pregnant. That doesn't mean that God is trying to "get" you. It's just a law of nature. You must choose to move forward in the grace that you will find in our Father.

I've formed a habit over the last few years. When I make a mistake, I genuinely ask forgiveness and ask the Lord to help me cultivate the fruit of the Spirit in my life. With the Spirit's fruit growing in me I will not easily fall into sin again. At that point I man-up and deal with any effects of my actions and then move forward. When the enemy tries to remind me of my mistakes, I remind him that I am the righteousness of God through Christ Jesus my Redeemer! I believe the Spirit of the Lord would say to you right now, "be free from your past, be free from your own thoughts that don't line up with God's Word, be free from condemnation! BE FREE!"

2. Love

First John 4:8 tells us that God is Love. This is not the perverted, manipulative, self-serving emotion that poses as love. The love that describes God is Agape love, as detailed in 1 Corinthians 13:1-13. Take a moment and read that passage. Replace the word love with God every time you see it. It's overwhelming! With God not only having the attributes of Agape love, but *being* these attributes, it's easy to see how He is for us and never against us. If the enemy can ever get us to doubt God's love for us, we will eventually doubt His promises to us.

The love I have for my children does not mean I always give in to their demands or that I never discipline them. I will not give my girls what I know they're not ready for or something that I know would harm them. Instead I observe their maturity level, their attitude, and their motive. I also discipline them when the situation calls for it. I do not discipline Julie in the same way I discipline Mackenzie. There is nearly 10 years difference in their ages. But I also don't reward them the same way. This doesn't mean that I love one more than the other. It means I love them individually. Riley, our middle daughter, had waited patiently (mostly) for her 10th birthday. The reason? She knew that Julie received a cell phone for her 10th birthday. No one ever told Riley that she was getting a cell phone. She assumed it. She talked about it as fact for 3 years. She knew that we would never do something for one we wouldn't do for another. But she also realized that she would have to come of age. Guess what she got for her birthday? She became the proud owner of a brand new cell phone. The unfortunate mindset that many believers have is that the Lord loves someone else more than them. The reality is that we are individuals to God and He will relate to us exactly that way. His love for us is so intense. As long as we have the "world-love" mindset we will never comprehend Agape love in its fullness.

Jesus told us that we would be given the Holy Spirit, who is the Spirit of Truth. He will help us understand the things of the Spirit that the world will never understand. Ask every day for the Spirit of Truth to help you see things through the love of God. When you do, you'll be able to rest in the understanding that your relationship with Him is bathed in that perfect love!

3. A rewarder of those who diligently seek Him

Maybe you've heard this truth. It's found in Hebrews 11:6. However, it doesn't just state that He rewards the diligent seeker. Let's read it together in the Amplified version:

"But without faith it is impossible to please God and be satisfactory to Him. For   whoever would come near to God must [necessarily] believe that God exists and that   He   is the rewarder of those who earnestly and diligently seek Him [out]."

It's not just saying that He rewards, but by faith we must believe who He is, and that He will reward us. Faith is the key component in our relationship with Christ from the beginning. We have to believe in our hearts and confess with our mouths to be saved (Romans 10:10). So why should it be any different as we walk further with the Lord? In order to know God as a rewarder, I had to believe that He was before He ever did. Make sense? As I seek Him, I know I will find Him. Every morning it's my practice to ask God for Divine wisdom, Divine protection, and to show me a sign of His Favor (Psalm 86:17). I believe and expect that He will and He always does! I believe that when I tithe, not only will God rebuke the devourer in my life, but He will open the windows of Heaven and pour out blessing in my life! I believe that when I praise Him, He will inhabit those praises! I believe that if I am faced with illness (no matter how small or large) I am healed by the blood of Jesus!

Never, never, never allow doubt to set up house in your heart! Stand on the truth of the Word and the Rewarder will show up in your life! As you begin to find out who God is to you, the influence of that knowledge will permeate every area of your life. People will recognize that you truly know the God you serve. If you have trouble in this area of your life, here are some tips that may help you:

- Have an accountability partner

  Not someone in your church. They may not "appreciate" that their pastor's wife has trouble reading her Bible and praying. Even if they have the same problem, in their mind, you are never to struggle with this. The best person may be a fellow minister's wife, your spouse, or if you're a staff wife, your pastor's wife.

- Journal

  This is a personal preference of mine. I began journaling when I was 15 and still practice it to this day. It not only makes me accountable to myself, but it's a great record of my spiritual journey. I sometimes write the day's events. Sometimes I write prayers. Other times, I simply jot down the passages I studied that day.

- Collect Bible study guides

  Many books today have study guides to assist the reader. This is a great way to stay on track with what you are studying.

- Listen to podcasts or preaching CD's

  As I exercise, clean my house, or take a long road trip, I am sure to have a podcast or a few CD's of my favorite ministers. It focuses my mind on the Word and allows me to grow spiritually even during the busiest days of my life.

Relationship #2: Your Marriage

I love my man, but between 3 kids, the church, my job, and extracurricular activities, things can get pretty hectic. He's a workaholic personality. I'm an artist. I like to go with the flow. He lives by his calendar. When these two worlds collide, it's not pretty. With that stated, Gladys Knight said it well: "I'd rather live in his world, than live without him in mine!" Mark and I both came from ministry families: two very different ministry families. I was a yeller, he was an ignorer. I was a brat, he was a know-it-all. Our first year of marriage was hell on earth. We were both out of control. Just before our first anniversary, everything came to a head. We were leaving for a missions trip and we decided that when we got back, that I would leave. We kept it quiet, but we were positive that this was the answer. That's when the Holy Spirit stepped into the picture. As He sweetly reminded us of the people we'd fallen in love with, we decided to go forward with our anniversary trip as a last ditch effort. It worked. When we returned home from our vacation, we were determined to see this marriage succeed. What it's taken is a lot of "on purpose" moments in our life. I had to learn that romance is sometimes planned for weeks in advance. I learned that just because Mark is in essence his own boss, he still has to go to work. He can't stay home and watch TV with me all day. And he had to learn that he could actually relax on his day off. Well, first he had to learn to take a day off. We learned that spending time together didn't always mean spending money. And I learned that being happy when he did something with the guys was very good for us! What I am saying is, Team Haston decided to be the best we could be! We still fuss, as all couples do, no matter what they say. I still try to boss him, and he still reminds me who is actually the boss. But overall, we have created a rhythm for our relationship. Believe me, if you don't create the rhythm, someone else will do it for you. It sounds really spiritual to some when you proclaim, "the Lord's work comes first! Hallelujah!!" But announcing your divorce from the pulpit? Not so spiritual. When my parents divorced after 32 years of marriage and full-time ministry, my marriage took on a whole new priority. You must have a healthy relationship with your husband in order to have a healthy ministry.

Here Are Some Things We've Discovered Over the Years:

1. Keep dating.

Keep dating each other, of course. Otherwise, you'll need to get a different kind of book. Mark and I were going through a super busy time at the church and personally when we implemented "date night" on a regular basis. We had always tried to work it into our schedules, but until we began putting it on the calendar, it was often overlooked. At this point in our lives, we have a 15 year old that helps with her sisters, so we can have a weekly date. It's every Thursday night, unless something unforeseen happens. Then we change it to Friday night. In the last 2 years, we have maybe missed date night five times. It's been glorious! It's only a couple of hours. We normally go eat (so we can talk) and then walk around somewhere. Mark has talked about it enough from the pulpit, that if we do run into someone from the church, they normally respect our privacy. I understand that everyone is at a different stage in life. So if once a week is impossible, go on a planned date at least once a month. This does not mean extravagance. It can be a simple meal at a simple place. Note: it's not a date if you invite your children or another couple go with you! You need time alone - just the two of you!

2. Take trips.

As I mentioned before, Mark and I took a trip for our first anniversary. We had free plane tickets and planned a thrifty trip to Cancun. It was great. We have not had the privilege of going on a big trip every anniversary since then, but we do try to get away at least 2-3 days a year. Mark is an online hotel shopping machine and we normally get away fairly inexpensively. We often go places that are drivable to save money, as well. These trips are some of the greatest memories we have together. We take lots of pictures and one day, I will make scrapbooks of our adventures. Ok, I probably won't, but at least we have the pictures. Our children are never invited on these trips, neither are our friends. It is time for just the two of us. We do our best not to discuss church issues and to plan activities that we enjoy doing together. We recently returned from one of these trips and thinking about it now makes me smile.

3. Be intimate...a lot!

If your children sleep with you, kick them out. Our bedroom is a sanctuary for us. I rarely even allow the girls to watch television in our room. That's mostly because I don't want to sleep on Pop-Tart crumbs, but you get what I'm saying. Intimacy in marriage is not only the act of sex, but the protection of the union it represents. When your husband is under a great deal of stress, he doesn't always want to talk it out. You know what I'm saying. Sex is a wonderful gift from God for the marriage covenant. It's a very important part of your relationship. It's healthy for your marriage to have sexual intimacy in some form or fashion on a regular basis. Please don't be a wife that withholds sex from your husband as a manipulation tool. Our society has made it some sort of stupid joke that "he" needs it, but "she" doesn't, so it rarely happens. And even then it is some sort of wifely duty. Men are physiologically created to need sex, but guess what? We can enjoy it and even "need" it too!

If you are genuinely having difficulty in your sexual relationship, make it a matter of prayer. Maybe you are physically exhausted at bedtime. Who wrote the rule that sex must be had at night in the dark? Lunch time may be the perfect time for you. You may possibly have a real physical issue that makes sex extremely painful or unfulfilling. It is still your responsibility as a wife to fulfill your husband's needs (and vice versa). Ask the Lord to help you be creative. Remember pornography or adding another person to the mix are not options for believers. The marriage bed is undefiled but opening the door to outside lust, adultery, or homosexuality is harmful and sinful no matter how private it may be. Once that is established, go for it! Find ways to be physically intimate. The book "Every Man's Battle" states that it only takes 72 hours of no sexual gratification for a man to begin to have physical and mental issues or temptation. God placed us together to fulfill needs in our spouse's life. If this is a problem area in your marriage, go to the Lord and to His Word. Begin to study out Agape love (1 Corinthians 13). Find out how to be a giver and how to crucify your flesh. Crucify your flesh?! Yes. That's right. Sex in the sacred borders of the marriage covenant is not only a physical act, but it is first and foremost a spiritual act. It is the physical consummation of a very spiritual covenant. God cares about every area of your life!

4. Guard your heart.

       The newest trend in adultery in the church seems to be the "emotional affair". I am not making light of this, I'm calling attention to what is becoming an epidemic in the church. It is especially being seen among ministers. It is as if we have enough self control to not cross the line sexually, but not enough wisdom to stay on the safe side emotionally. Proverbs speaks extensively about wisdom. Proverbs also speaks extensively about the adulterous woman. It's no coincidence, I assure you. Another thing I can assure you of is you will have times in your marriage that one or both of you are not having a need met. It is in these times that life altering decisions can be made. Proverbs 9:1-12 describes how wisdom cries out to all those who need her, but check out verses 13-18. It's folly calling out, almost identically, to those who don't know any better. Mark and I have made a commitment to ask the Lord everyday for divine wisdom in every area of our lives, including our marriage. James 1:5 admonishes us that if we lack wisdom, ask for it. And when you do, God will give it to you liberally! Guarding your heart is a choice. You cannot say you got in over your head before you knew it, if you are asking for wisdom every day. Wisdom will give you special insight into the people around you. You will see motives and attitudes that may not have been apparent before. In our marriage, we have allowed the other person permission to point out wolves. This is not a jealousy license - it's trust in the other's discernment. It began when we first married and continues to this day. If we ever argue about the opinion, that's a red flag to check our own motives. I do not confide in any person of the opposite sex about anything! When it comes to our marriage, I have no business degrading my husband to anyone. I went through counseling after my parent's divorce with a counselor whom my husband first approved. We also have an unwritten rule that we don't make fun of one another from the pulpit. We tell stories about personal experiences, and they are often humorous, but we never say anything about the other that could be seen as degrading or disrespectful. We are seen as a united team in every area. We have a lot of fun publicly and don't mind being discreetly affectionate. No one is going to be invited into our secret world…including you. So that's all I'll say about that.

Relationship #3: Your Children

PK's (preacher's kids, for those of you just joining us) have been marked as wild, rebellious, deceitful, sinful, and on and on. I, for one, do not like it one bit! I did my fair share of living up to those labels, but I don't believe my children have to be prodigals in order to be normal. The sad thing is that many church members like to make these jokes and pick on PK's whether they are good kids or not. It is our responsibility to protect the hearts of our children from the cradle to the day they leave the nest. By that I mean we have to let their eyes be open to the realities of the ministry without making them bitter and resentful. My parents generally did a good job of this. Sometimes they talked in front of me a little too much, something I've been guilty of as well. But when I left the house, I was honored that the Lord had chosen me to continue in the ministry. I wasn't scared or jaded or bitter. I was keenly aware of some of the things that were ahead, but I was still very happy about "The Call". I want my girls to look back on our life with no regrets of being a PK. I want them to be thrilled that their daddy was a preacher man!

How Can You Raise Healthy PK's?

1. Be their parents, then their pastors.

In our house a common phrase is used: "It's not because your dad is the Pastor, it's because we're believers." We want them to know that the moral and spiritual standards that we adhere to are because we love the Lord. People's opinions are secondary. We have certain rules and guidelines that would be there if Mark was a plumber. It just is what it is. We don't ignore the fact, however, that we are to be examples and that people are watching us more than others. We try to major on the majors and minor on the minors. This is becoming more of an issue right now with our oldest, Julie, simply because she is now in the youth group and in public ministry. She joined the choir as soon as she went to Jr. High. I asked her to be a leader in worship because several of her friends joined the choir as well. Julie is a born leader and I knew that if she raised her hands during worship, paid attention during practice, and generally took things seriously, the others would follow suit. We began to see this happen as we believed it would. I wasn't putting her on display. I was simply asking her to use the gifting God had given her for a noble purpose. On the other hand, she wore black nail polish one Sunday because it matched her outfit. This was met with some dislike on the part of some prying church members. When a "ha-ha" comment was made to me about it, I let them know immediately (in love, of course) that I had purchased the polish myself and was considering it for my next manicure. I was very kind about it, but when I verbally put myself on her side, silly opinions backed down. She was no longer embarrassed and she knew that we were in her corner. Our girls know when push comes to shove, we pick them...all day, every day!

2. Make time for them.

Mark's day off is Friday. During the summer, Friday is called family day. During the school year, Friday night is family night. They occasionally spend the night with friends, but generally it's spent as the Haston 5! We do things like walk in the nostalgic downtown area of our town or run to a neighboring city for the day. We go to movies that they've been waiting to see or watch recorded episodes of family friendly TV shows. Often at the dinner table, we have a time for "High / Low". Each one of us tells our high and low for that day. Our youngest, Mackenzie, is six. She usually says something like

"My high is I love Disney World and my low is that I got a boo-boo on my ankle". And then she laughs hysterically. It makes no sense, but for a couple of minutes she has the complete attention of the entire family. We find out what happened at school that day or what boy is trying to call one of our daughters. It makes us, as parents, approachable. Kenzie's low may be a boo-boo today, but in ten years, she'll feel comfortable enough to tell us that she's feeling overwhelmed or upset. We want the girls to understand now that they are so important to us, that what they have to say is important, and how they are feeling is important. They know that unless Mark is in a crisis counseling session, his door is always open to them, even if it's literally closed at the time. He's their daddy at the church just like he's their daddy at home. Our middle daughter, Riley, has started her own Sunday night tradition. She rides home with Mark by herself after service. He tells me she sits right in the middle of his front seat and snuggles up next to him. She then proceeds to talk incessantly until they arrive in our driveway 15 minutes later. It's her time alone with him. And he loves it.

3. Take a family vacation.

The greatest memories of my childhood are of our annual family vacation to the beach. My parents bought a time share in 1982. We went every summer for the rest of my years at home. When Mark and I married in 1994, the tradition continued! The trip would cost us gas money and groceries while we were there. We cooked all our meals in the condo and did nothing but go out to the ocean every day. I cannot imagine my life without those memories. We have chosen to do the same thing with our girls. We take a family vacation every year. Some years we have had to be incredibly thrifty, but the girls had no idea. And now, without hesitation, they ask what we are doing for our summer trip. We often go with cousins and grandparents, but never with anyone else. It's important for us to have a time of healthy separation from our church family. As much as we love them, our girls deserve a week of no one but us!

4. They are PK's, not church property.

Just because you and your husband are "hired" by a particular church, your children do not become property of the church. It's like living in a parsonage (which I am thrilled to say, we no longer do). It's your house, right? But somehow, someway a precious saint at a ladies tea you're hosting will be sure to give you her opinion of your freshly painted bathroom. "Hmmm, Did the board give permission for such a buttery yellow to be used on church property?" When actually, the board gave you Carte' Blanche' to make this public place home to your family. The same will be done by every Tattle-Telly Nelly that decides they are pretty sure they saw your child roll her eyes at them or bite their precious Suzy-Q in the nursery. Ok, well that last part is true about Mackenzie, but that's neither here nor there! Your children need to know rules and boundaries just as any child does, but they do not need to constantly be the living example of discipline in the church. Our staff wives, an adopted grandmother named Mrs. Barbara, and our lead nursery attendant are allowed to spank Mackenzie at the church. They have been in her life for her entire life. They love her like family, but if anyone else sees her being disobedient, they are to tell me or they will deal with me. When she was born, Mark announced to the church on a Sunday morning that I would be bringing her to service that night. And with humor he told them that she was like the Hope

Diamond. They could look, but could not touch. This was a funny and kind way of saying, she may be the most "famous" baby in the church, but she's our baby. Don't put your dirty hands on her! No one was offended, but they all got the message. Teach your children respect for authority, but don't allow them to be bullied just because everyone knows them.

5. Speak highly of your church whenever possible.

Any time someone in the church gives a gift card to a restaurant, we are sure to tell the girls that the meal we are enjoying is a gift from someone. After Pastor Appreciation Sunday or our birthday party given by the church, we make it a point to "appreciate" God's people verbally to our children. They need to know that church members are our family not our foe!

NOTE: Those birthday parties were begun by us and carried on by kind people. They have been taught to celebrate their pastor. Now it comes to them naturally!

Relationship #4: The Church Staff

Ahhh....staff. We've had the good, the bad, and the ugly. We, too, were on staff under two pastors at the same church. The pastor who hired us, left for a position in our state office. His successor was kind enough to allow us to stay. The same church with two completely different leadership styles, it was a learning experience for sure. After 2 years of staff ministry, we accepted the Senior Pastorate at our first church. The church was not financially able to handle paid staff in the beginning. So we worked with an all volunteer staff. Many of us will have to do this at some point in your ministry and are possibly there now. It is very different than full-time paid staff. They are exhausted from working a secular job. You will have to be patient with them, as they will many times be late or just on time for certain events. The key to volunteer staff is appreciation. They want to help you or they wouldn't be there. Be kind to them, but don't allow them to manipulate you because of their extenuating circumstances. A little known fact: you can fire volunteers. It's true! Many pastors feel caught in a trap because these people are doing this work "as unto the Lord. Hallelujah." The enemy can send distractions to you through volunteers. We'll talk more about that later, but for now, let's focus on full-time staff relationships.

This culture of reality TV that we live in has caused drama to be something that is expected when you get any group of people together. The Word says in Romans 12:18, "if it is at all possible, live peaceably with all men". Among believers, it is possible to live in peace, but it's a choice. We are all serving the Prince of Peace. Peace is one of the fruit of the Spirit. You would think we would be choosing peace. You would think. I like peace much more than drama and strife. So, we do everything we can to keep peace among our staff. Mark is a strong leader, but he is also a learner. He has learned over the years that to be a strong leader doesn't necessarily mean leading with a strong arm. He also understands that every staff member has a different personality and a different way of needing motivation. He expects diligence from our staff, but understands that they are just as human as he is.

Lessons We Have Learned

1. Respect is a two-way street.

If you'll respect your staff for what they bring to the table, it will be easier for them to respect you. If you could do everything they do, then why did you hire them? Mark doesn't want to lead worship, preach in youth, and teach kid's church. That's why we have assembled a fabulous team of Godly, talented people. As the pastor's wife, I have a responsibility to promote unity and respect among the staff wives. We appreciate and often compliment one another for the jobs we are all doing. Before I was on paid staff, I was very involved in our music department. I had a close working relationship with our former Worship Pastor. His wife knew every time that we met, made a decision, or spoke on the phone. She knew that I respected her as his wife and never wanted her to feel like I was overstepping my bounds. Because of this, we were a great team.

2. The staff who plays together, stays together.

Several years ago, we started a Tuesday staff meeting. Mark felt that the wives may have been feeling left out, so he invited us in for a short "Let's get on the same page meeting." It eventually evolved into staff lunch on Tuesdays at 11:45. We talked a little business, but you know what it primarily revolved around? Just relaxing conversation. It gives everyone a chance to be heard and to catch up. Sundays at church are very busy. Some of us have small children, so we rarely eat together after service. Instead, we set aside this Tuesday lunch to bond. This is not a time to go over church business. We talk about silly things like one husband eating his pregnant wife's leftover steak, to major family rifts that are occurring in their extended families. We also have an occasional fajita night at our house (because I make the best guacamole!). One of our favorite events with one staff team was the annual "All-Church Thanksgiving Dinner Staff Video". It began completely by accident when we were trying to come up with some form of entertainment and turned into a much anticipated treat! We tried to out-do ourselves every year and that was pretty hard because we had made some funny videos. It was just a wonderful break in the holiday rush that we looked forward to each year.

3. Spiritual accountability is crucial.

Not only does Mark ask the guys to turn in accountability forms, but he completes one as well. We want the spiritual temperature of our church to be hot and we understand it begins with the leadership. Our wives are not forced into any type of ministry, but are strongly encouraged to find their passion and go for it! We are all involved in the worship service, altar time, and special prayer time. We ask one another often what we are studying or reading or watching. We fast together and share prayer needs with one another. As much fun as we have together, we know that we are on a mission. And we never want to leave a man behind!

As the pastor's wife, you have a great responsibility to keep a finger on the pulse of your staff wives. One of my greatest regrets as a pastor's wife was ignoring little signs of big problems. If your staff never invites you or other people to their home, maybe you should ask why. If you know that your church is taking care of them financially, but they seem to be in constant financial difficulties, ask why. If you sense constant strain in their marriage relationship, ask why. If the anointing

29

on their life begins to lift, ask why. I cannot stress enough the importance of this point! The word says that it's the small foxes that spoil the vine. If you feel that there is tension between your staff wives or even ungodly attitudes toward you and your husband, take care of it! It would be better to discipline or even let a staff member go, than to allow sinful behavior or dishonorable actions in your leadership. I'd rather deal with one or two couples than to allow rebellion in the camp and it ultimately affect our entire congregation. Being the leader means your *right* decisions may not always be the most popular decisions. But righteous leaders will always be rewarded with righteous followers!

4. If needed...jump ship.

If you are a staff wife reading this book, please convey this message to your husband. If ever the time comes that you cannot line up with the vision of the Senior Pastor, leave. The Lord did not call you where you are to:

- Stir up strife among people around you

- Hang around until the old guy leaves so you can step in

- Stay with a man who is not hearing from God

If things aren't jiving, you are to be the one to leave. If the pastor should go, that is between him and the church board. If you are supposed to go back, they'll call you. It's that simple. Consider David. He had been anointed king even while Saul was on the throne. Did he push his way into the palace? No. He ran for his life. He knew that it would never be right to stretch his hand out toward God's man. Saul had long since lost the anointing, but David still respected the office. God blessed David for his servant's heart.

Relationship #5: The People in Your Church

I will speak quickly on this subject since there are more chapters to address church people in your life. However, it is a good idea to note a few things when it comes to personal relationships with your church members.

1. You can't be BFF's with church members.

For those of you unfamiliar with the reality TV show, "I Want to be Paris Hilton's New BFF" or something like that, it stands for Best Friends Forever. I just heard a gasp! Someone reading this just said, "How dare you tell me who my friends can be!" And to that, I ask you to put yourself in another church member's shoes. Not the one who would hate you no matter what, but the quiet one, who would love to take you to lunch but doesn't want to "impose." Of course there are people in my church with whom I have more in common. Our lifestyles, children, ages, and many things we may have in common. There are even people I have nothing in common with, I just enjoy their company. Here is the simple truth: you are going to be closer to some more than others. Your responsibility then turns to not making it a big deal. Don't sit just with your friends during service. I promise it will hurt someone's feelings whether they say it does or not. This may seem trivial to you, but the Word tells us to "give no place to the Devil". If he can plant the word "favoritism" in someone's mind, then you have a problem. We choose, as staff wives, to sit together on the front row. It's not to be exclusionary, it's to show unity to the church and support to our husbands. The other wives are allowed to sit with their ministry if they choose (i.e. the youth pastor's wife with the youth group). Otherwise, we don't make a practice of sitting with certain people. It also allows the church to see the wives worship and have a supportive attitude during the service, as well as, be right near the altar area, should someone need prayer. This has worked well for us, but you can modify the idea to fit your church. We also choose to disperse ourselves as much as possible at other church functions, such as women's meetings. We try to all sit with different women that we might not get a chance to visit with otherwise. I assure you that people are watching how much time you spend with other members. Celebrate the relationships that God has given you in the church, but be respectful of the feelings of the flock to which you're assigned to minister.

2. Keep confidential church business confidential.

There will be times when people in the church will have to be disciplined for one reason or the other. There will be times when one staff member is not getting along so great with the other. Keep these matters private! Yes, we must be authentic and transparent. But Proverbs 17:9 reminds us, "He who covers a transgression seeks love, but he who repeats a matter separates friends." This certainly doesn't mean to *cover up* sin, rather do your best to allow people to work out their issues in private if at all possible.

Mark and I have come to understand this can also mean protecting these people even from your staff. Sometimes your staff members may not be able to handle negative information about church members or even one another. The information may cause them to hold a grudge toward someone especially if it involves words spoken against leadership in some emotional rant. Or your staff may not be mature enough to handle a "juicy tidbit" about someone. We bring the staff in on situations only when necessary.

The same is true for the board. If it is not a matter that would necessitate the board's actions, then there is no reason to bring shame to someone who is repentant and has a teachable spirit. If the discipline calls for someone to step down from a ministry or leadership position for a season, Mark relates this to our board with as much privacy as possible for the offender. We are not in the business of embarrassing people or publicly calling them out. We simply follow biblical protocol for church discipline.

Of course it is obviously never appropriate to discuss issues concerning one church member with another. I love the statement Mark makes at the beginning of a counseling session or meeting about spiritual correction: "Your situation is not worth losing my ministry." In essence what he is telling them is they can be assured that we will keep their confidential matters confidential. That one "secret" could cost us the trust of people and lead to the loss of our influence. Ministry is about influence. When you lose trust and influence with the people God has given you to shepherd, you have lost your ability to minister to them. He has called us to love people as He loves people. Having them feel safe under the umbrella of your leadership is a beautiful expression of that love!

One way you can practice confidentiality is to remain quiet about things that are still in the planning stages of the operation of the church. For example, we do what we refer to as Christmas Miracles each year. All of the staff is normally aware of what will be presented to particular families at our big reveal service, but how disappointing would it be for one of us to blab the surprise before it can happen? We've given away cars, thousands of dollars, and amazing gifts over the years. Each time we reveal the blessing to the family in front of our congregation, we get a genuine reaction for everyone to enjoy including the recipient. I love that! So be careful how much you tell even of the direction you feel the Lord taking your congregation and shout it from the roof tops only when it is the appointed time. When you speak things at the right time, it fits just as the Lord planned it to fit. Learning to keep confidences is one of the wisest things you can do as a woman in ministry!

CHAPTER 2

Finding Your Place

In writing this book, I have probably been the most excited about this chapter! The reason? I dealt with this issue for several years. When I was a little girl, my parents shifted from a mainstream denomination to the non-denominational arena. They always believed and supported women being in ministry and leadership. In the early part of their ministry, the denomination they belonged to seemed to have more than their share of ladies who were the scary mountain-women types. You know...hairy legs, raspy voices? So it wasn't exactly super-appealing to my 4'10" (and ½)...that's for you, Mom...my cute little mama! I am glad to tell you that I soon realized that the same anointing that the old-time holiness mothers of our faith preached under could rest on exhorters, teachers, singers, & even the quiet ones among us!

God has a specific call and purpose for you. It will always complement your husband's ministry, not compete with it! As my parents moved into different circles, they began to see minister's wives who had more of a teaching ministry. This is where my mother found her niche. My mom was a singer, not a speaker...in her eyes. But the Lord had a greater purpose than she realized. Mom was an intercessor and as she prayed one day, she saw something in the Spirit. I want you to understand that the pictures we see in our mind's eye are often put there by the Holy Spirit. One example of this is during Abram's conversation with Jehovah God. He was told to look around him and everything he could see, he could have

(Genesis 13:14-18)! We can't take for granted what God tells us to see in our spirit man. What Mom saw in her spirit was from the Lord. As she was praying, she saw herself in a large ballroom filled with women. The room had a support column right in the middle of it and on the front row was an African American woman in an orange outfit. My mother saw herself on the platform speaking. The details were so clear that she even recognized the dress she was wearing to speak in was a dress she already owned. Remember, she wasn't a speaker but immediately she knew this was from the Lord! At the time, the Women's Aglow organization was quite large in the Memphis area where I was raised. Not long after Mom saw this picture in her spirit, she received a phone call asking her to speak at the next Aglow meeting. She quickly said yes even though it was an intimidating thought to her. She wore the dress that she'd seen herself in, just in case it meant something. But when she stood on the platform of the large ballroom where the meeting was being held, there in the middle of the room stood a support column and on the front row sat the African American lady dressed in orange! WOW! That is how God wants us to experience our dreams! He wants the dreams, visions, and plans He places deep within us to be so real in our Spirit that when we see it with our physical eyes, it's just déjà vu!

What do you see yourself doing? Are you a successful business woman, a Bible teacher, preacher, stylist, mommy, singer? You know one of the things I saw myself doing? Writing this book! I have tears in my eyes just sitting in this moment! Whatever your dream is, you can achieve it! There is no right or wrong dream. I mean, sister, with the exception of wanting to be an exotic dancer or a bank robber, you can be anything and bring glory to God! The cool thing about seeking first the Kingdom of God in your life is that all the things you desire will line up with His will! Psalm 37:3-5 says to trust in the Lord, delight yourself in Him, and commit your ways to Him. The Amplified Bible says that when you do these things, "He will give you the desires and secret petitions of your heart. When you trust Him He will bring these things to pass." That's the beauty of aligning yourself with the Lord. His will becomes your will. As exciting as all these things are, there is always order to God's purpose. We must have zeal and wisdom!

Can You See It?

As I mentioned before, God told Abram that all the land he saw he could and would have! But when God told him that he would be the father of nations? Now that was a different story. He argued with God "Don't you know how old I am?" Sarah just laughed. Don't be mean to Sarah because, honey child, if I was an old woman I might laugh too! But the truth still stands: "With God ALL things are possible!" Abraham and Sarah had their moments. That Hagar/Ishmael thing wasn't one of their finest. But the book of Romans says Abraham didn't weaken in faith when he thought about their aged bodies. No unbelief or distrust made him waver concerning the promises of God (Romans 4:19-20). When God places a dream or desire inside of you, you'll be given plenty of opportunities to dismiss them. Whether it's your own insecurities, people around you, or overwhelming circumstances, the choice is yours to hold tight to the dream!

Everyone understands that arrogant people are full of pride, but do you realize that insecurity is rooted in pride as well? Insecurity says "I can never be good enough. I don't have the talent or education of others in this field. I'm not as pretty. I don't have the right clothes. My house isn't as nice. I'm not outgoing enough." Insecurity says, "Not even God Himself

37

could qualify me to do what He's asking me to do!" I just felt you wince while reading that last part. Maybe you would never speak those words, but guess what? Every time you allow insecurity to speak for you, that's exactly what you're saying. If you say "no" to a dream because of insecurity, you are in essence saying, "The Lord God who can do anything isn't powerful enough to prepare me for the purposes to which He is calling me." And because of the nature of God, He will not force you to do anything. He will simply raise up a willing vessel to complete His will. I have put so many things off because of my prideful insecurities. I was terribly convicted one day while reading a book by Dr. Mike Murdock. It was the simple statement that delayed obedience is disobedience. It hit me between the eyes. I was the queen of excuses that all stemmed from insecurity and fear. I talked a big game but never acted on it and then would get upset when someone else showed up doing my idea! Why? Because I knew it was my fault. I didn't truly believe God could bring to pass what He was calling me to do. Some of my insecurities came from my concern of what other people thought of me. I had many colleagues who chose not to participate in the ministry in the same way that I was driven to. They were involved in ministry and loved people. They were in right relationship with God, but when I expressed some desire to teach or preach, they turned up their noses. I began to hide my work when one of my close friends made fun of me for writing songs. She said sarcastically "What are you, a song writer?!" And then she laughed and added "You'll probably be preaching next!" I've had choir directors take solos from me in the middle of choir practice because I was "outdoing" the second verse soloist. I found myself shrinking into my own world full of unfulfilled dreams and that was the place my spirit began to shut down. That's what happens when you stifle your gifts.

The day came when I remembered my mom's vision. She used to tell me before she prayed over me at night, "Cheree', God has made you a leader." My earliest memory of this was when I was six years old but it stuck with me. My mom went on to be a sought-after speaker in the church and business world. She speaks to this day. God has promoted her because of her ability to see things in the Spirit. Her example has caused me to make a concerted effort to "own" the pictures in my mind of lovely, pure, just, noble, and good report thoughts (Philippians 4:8)! Last year I recorded my very first "live" CD. It has been a dream of mine for five years. When I took the platform I was almost overwhelmed that the dream I'd seen so many times with my faith eyes was now right in front of my physical eyes! We have to understand something. Our faith eyes have to be more real than our physical eyes. If God spoke the worlds into existence, then what actually existed first? The Spirit, not the physical! Romans 4:17 says that God calls into existence those things that don't exist (in the physical) as though they do exist. Second Corinthians 4:18 says, "We do not look at the things which are seen, but at the things which are not seen. For the things which are seen are temporary, but the things which are not seen are eternal." God's purposes are eternal, not my lack of _____ (fill in the blank)! Moses stuttered and was a murderer, yet God chose him to deliver His people out of bondage!

Joyce Meyer's testimony is such an inspiration to me. She was sexually abused by her own father. By her own admission she was a smoking, angry, know-it-all with a big mouth! She may have been all those things, but let me add one more: She was willing and obedient to walk in God's purpose for her life. And would you look at what God decided to do with that! The Lord is simply asking you to be obedient. I promise if you say "yes", He will give you the plan, the people, and the resources you will need to complete the task.

A funny thing happened when I said "yes" to writing this book. I sat down the first day and for the next NINE hours wrote out the first chapter. It was a wonderfully anointed God-moment. I thought to myself "This is going to be a cinch! I'll have this book written in no time." Then my life showed up the next day. I'm a mom, a wife, a friend, a Realtor (yep, it's true), a sister, a minister, an astronaut...Ok, not so much an astronaut, but you get the picture. Something demanded my time and attention every day. I began to wonder if I'd ever get to chapter two. Well, my real estate business began to slow to nearly a halt so I made the decision to substitute teach in the higher grades of my daughter's school district. I was very discouraged one day and asked the Lord why He was not working on my behalf in real estate. Why was I having to substitute teach? This was His reply: "Didn't you ask me for time to write your book? I'm trying to give you several uninterrupted hours with no phone, no Facebook, no email so you can focus your mind and write. Not only am I giving you that time, but you are being paid to do it." It was one of those speechless moments. Oh my goodness. I was about to get paid to write my book. So as I wrote the first draft of this second chapter, I was sitting in a seventh grade reading class. They were quiet and did their assignments. They had no idea that an anointed woman of God was sitting behind them writing out her destiny! I have chosen to see myself through God's purposes for me! God wants you to do the same. Can you see it?

Shut Yo' Mouth Josephina!

I love to talk. Talk, talk, talk, talk, talk! It doesn't really matter what subject. If I'm in the mood, it's on! But when it's something I'm passionate about? Oh, watch out now! One deep breath and I can go for hours. For a talker, the lessons learned about talking too much are hard ones. What "my people" don't always see (until it's too late) is that talking too much can be obnoxious and annoying. The listeners sometimes peg you as a story-stacker (you'll not find that word in the dictionary. I made it up.). Story-stackers are people who begin sentences with the phrase, "Oh, yeah, that's nothing - listen to this!" Talkers may not mean to brag or story-stack. They just want to keep saying words. Talkers are usually also interrupters (not sure of the validity of that word either - oh well). It's not that they are always selfish, they're just overly excited!

The Lord had to teach me to shut my mouth. I learned to shut my mouth while talking to Him, talking to my family, and talking to people in general. I had to learn to listen. Talking is needed. I'm outgoing and a good communicator. That comes from all my talking experience! But talking also made some people not care too much for me. The worst part of talking too much was that it gave my enemies ammunition. I realized this while reading the story of Joseph. He wasn't just a talker, but a dreamer as well. When a dreamer talks it makes non-dreamers really nervous. When God begins to reveal to you His plans for your life, remember not everyone will be happy for you. When people have the wrong mindset they somehow think the blessings that you receive came at their expense. They think the God who owns it all doesn't have enough for them. So our best course of action is to keep things to ourselves or have a very select few with whom we share our deepest heart thoughts. This doesn't mean that the time to tell will never come. However, we must wait for the right time. The reason this Old Testament story made such an impact on me is because I can sympathize with Joseph. He was a dreamer. I am a dreamer. He was a talker. I am a talker. He was his parent's favorite child. I am…well you get the picture. My sisters may read this and I don't like to cause strife. Basically, Joseph spoke before he thought. His brothers were already angry about his beautiful coat and then he decided to tell them of a dream he had where they all bowed down to him! Gee, I can see how they weren't too excited.

Everyone has a specific destiny. Some destinies just appear more glittery and sparkly than others. So when you hear the end of a thing, what is often overlooked is the path that gets you there. Someone introduces themselves as doctor so and so, and often we automatically think money and prestige. What you don't think about immediately are the years and years of studies and disciplines it took to be a doctor. How many successful people tell stories of their humble beginnings? Joseph's brothers did eventually bow before him but he was only in the palace after he'd been through the pit and the prison. Some may say that if Joseph had never told his dream that his brothers would've never sold him, thus he would've never ended up in the palace. Not necessarily true. God gave him that dream. Joseph was the one to make the mistake. Who's to say that Joseph's own family couldn't have been the providers through that famine? Who knows but God Himself? Joseph made a wrong choice and so did his brothers, but God's mercy prevailed for them all! We see at the end of the story that Joseph had learned his lesson. The talker knew when to be quiet. His brothers showed up in Egypt to ask for help. The Word says that Joseph didn't reveal who he was to them immediately. He did it at the right time and the right place. Proverbs has a lot to say about your mouth. Proverbs

17:28 says, "even a fool is seen as wise if they keep quiet." Proverbs 18:21 says, "the power of life and death are in the tongue!" The book is full of practical wisdom for us in so many areas, but especially about our speech!

Please understand that if I told all my dreams some people would think that I had lost my mind. When you take hold of dreams, God gives you even bigger ones. This book has been a dream of mine, but I couldn't tell everyone or I would've heard all the reasons why not to write it. I have dreams of where it will go, but now is not the time to announce it. My husband knows and a few others know. So who are those others? They are the handful of people in my life who I trust to always believe in me, pray for me, and encourage me. They are also the people who tell me the truth in love. They push and press me to be everything I am destined to be through Christ. They don't accept my excuses and they call me out when I need it. Ask God to reveal those people in your life to you. They are a beautiful gift. They are the people in my life that I can share my dreams with…'cause after all, a talker's got to talk!

Timing is Everything

Since I was a young girl, I dreamed of singing for millions and traveling in ministry. I also dreamed of getting married and having babies. As I got older I knew I would marry someone in full time ministry, probably a pastor. Those are all wonderful dreams. However, if the timing was off they would mix like oil and water.

I did marry that pastor and we did have those babies. For my situation and our personalities, my traveling to sing and speak all the time would have been a hindrance instead of a blessing. My girls needed me and still do today. I am an active participant in pastoring with my husband. I teach a large adult class, help direct the choir, greet the people during service and help our worship pastor with praise and worship. Our church is only now at a place that my absence wouldn't leave a gaping hole. Not because I'm so great, but because those things have been my divine assignments. On a personal level, I needed to grow more in the Word and in my relationship with Christ. I couldn't give what I didn't have myself. I've traveled sporadically through the years but I wouldn't have ministered with the effectiveness I can now after having walked through so many learning experiences. To be honest, I'm sure I'll look back fifteen years from now and see how much more I needed to learn!

Ecclesiastes says that there is a time and a season for everything. I was there for my girls' first steps, first words, and first birthdays. I was with Mark when we became pastors. I've sat in ladies' meetings (the good and the bad). I've been there for funerals, weddings and babies being born. I never want that part of my life to change because I enjoy it, but sometimes you have to give up something to have something else. I will always be a present wife and mother. My family is my first commitment. But my husband loves me too much to allow me to use him or the girls as an excuse to not go after my dreams. My priorities must be in the right place. If it's all about me, me, me - then the people in my life are neglected. If it's all about them, them, them - then God's purposes for me are neglected. Either way someone has the opportunity to become bitter and unfulfilled.

I must pause and make a point to those of you who are not yet married. First, marriage is a good thing if you marry the right person. There is partnership and companionship. The sense of "team" that I feel in my family cannot be matched! It begins with the head of our house, my husband, Mark. From the very beginning of our life together (including dating) he has been my biggest fan. He has pushed me through my paralysis of insecurity. He encourages me to soar! I once asked him how he would feel if I made more money than he made. You know what he said? He said, "That would be AWESOME!" And he meant it. He is a very strong man and a strong leader. At our church he is the pastor and I am his partner. Some people call me Pastor Cheree' and he is not bothered by it at all because he is secure in who he is. If you are dating or engaged to someone who doesn't want their wife in highly visible ministry, and you feel directed that way, you should probably rethink your relationship. Some men want and need a behind-the-scenes kind of woman. There is absolutely <u>nothing</u> wrong with that scenario. But if that is not who you are, you will be miserable! Mark respects the call of God on my life and I respect his authority. It is a glorious unity of ministry that the Lord has helped us create.

As the seasons of our lives have changed, so have our attitudes toward the ministry. It's not a job to us. It is something that neither of us could live without. Throughout our years together I've been sure God had forgotten us a few times, but alas, I was wrong...again. It just wasn't the right time. I decided several years ago that I would like to get my real estate license. I had all the paper work lined up to take my classes when I began to feel very sick. I thought I had a terrible flu. It wasn't the flu. It was a baby. All up in my 30 year old womb! What in the world was happening?! So there it was. I was pregnant. The $400 I had saved for my real estate classes went straight to my OBGYN since we didn't have maternity insurance. Disappointed, I was sure this was my time, but the Lord who knows the end from the beginning had my best interests in mind. Although Mark and I were not planning on having more children, Mackenzie was the greatest surprise we've ever received. You see, about a month after we got the news of the pregnancy, we received news of my parent's plan to divorce. I never realized that I was about to walk into the most difficult season of my life. Mackenzie proved to be a wonderful distraction for my family in what was otherwise a tragic time. Mackenzie is certainly the craziest, silliest, and most energetic of our three girls. She needed LOTS of attention as a baby and I was happy to give it to her. She is pure joy with skin on! I did eventually get my real estate license. God doesn't want you to give up on your dreams if unforeseen circumstances occur. He wants you to trust Him. His timing is always perfect!

As I stated earlier I recently recorded my first "live" CD. I've dreamed of it for years, but year after year things just never worked out. I was feeling discouraged because it was a huge undertaking. I'd had everyone I wanted to be a part of it in mind for a long time. I had worked and ministered with many musicians and singers. I'd picked out those who I thought would blend well. For one reason or another everyone changed directions. Some people left my life and some people walked into it. I asked the Lord why I was feeling separated from a particular few to whom I'd always been close. The Holy Spirit simply answered me with this statement "I'm closing doors behind you so you will walk through the open ones in front of you." It doesn't mean I wasn't sad in some ways or grieved with the loss of what those relationships had been, but I recognized that I was using those relationships as a crutch to stay in the background. God was moving me to the foreground. He was surrounding me with people who were right for this season of my life. As we planned the recording, I looked up to realize that the perfect team had been assembled. We had a glorious time of worship and I'm so glad it happened in God's

time, not mine. Psalm 46:10 "Be still and know that I am God.
I will be exalted among the nations! I will be exalted in the
earth!"

Do You Have What It Takes?

In this American Idol crazed culture, I am amazed at
the people who think that they are fabulous singers! How is it
that William Hung was signed to a recording contract and I
was beaten by a clown/monkey act at the America's Got Talent
audition in Dallas, TX? That is a shame. It is also true. There is
nothing wrong with exploring the options of open doors. If I
could get exposure as a minister and for our church, it would
be great! I assure you I had no plans of moving to Las Vegas to
star in a one woman show, "Cheree' Sings Elvis' Gospel
Favorites!" I just thought it would be a cool experience. So I
flew with my mom and her husband to Dallas for the auditions.
As we sat at dinner I said, "You know I understand there will
be a million singers here. As long as I don't get cut in round
one, then it's cool, unless I get beaten by a monkey or
something crazy!" Then I laughed and laughed. I guess Jesus
thought that would be funny, too. I made it through two
rounds beating roughly 1,000 singers. Round 3 however,
included talent from tap dancing to blowing up balloons with
your nose. Eeewww! It also included animal acts. There I was
in the audition room. I belted out my rendition of Aretha
Franklin's "Natural Woman". I was sure the judges would be
in awe or at the very least, be doubled over in tears. Instead,
they just stared at me. Then the mean British one (I couldn't
make this stuff up) says, "Thank you. You will not be moving
on." They didn't even break it to me gently. He just said it. I
was just telling my mom the news when over my shoulder I
heard congratulations being given to a round little clown

with... (Wait for it)...a MONKEY on her shoulder! I was appalled! I was honestly beaten by a monkey!

My Sunday school class thinks that this is the funniest story they've ever heard. I think they are mean. But seriously, sister friends, I was out of my element! "Natural Woman" may be my go-to karaoke song, but there's no anointing there. I am a minister, not a singer. *The song* just happens to be the way I minister at times. Until you recognize your true gifting, you could end up sounding like William Hung. You just won't fit. Let me insert a little advice for the sake of all mankind: Please, I beg you, do not sing if you sound like a dying cat! Lots of minister's wives sing, so it has become almost expected that they should all sing. It is NOT TRUE, I tell you! If I hear one more person say, "Well, my mama says I'm a good singer!" or "Sister Lula Bell says I always bless her with my voice!" I'm going to scream! Your mama has to say that and Sister Lula Bell is 96 and half deaf! Girl, put that "El Shaddai" soundtrack away and move on to something you're actually good at doing!

I would LOVE to be a professional organizer. Seriously, but y'all, I can hardly keep my side of the closet clean. It's weird. I'm a clean freak but I have to work to be organized. It's not a natural gift for me. It is for my husband, however. The parts of my life that are well organized are because of his influence on me. I love the finished product but the process of getting there is so stressful to me.

That's the difference in ability and a gift. I am able to organize anything but it doesn't come naturally. Decorating on the other hand I could do in my sleep. I love it! It's fun and actually relieves stress for me. Singing? Not a problem. Let me hear a song three times and I've got it. It's as natural as breathing. What are those gifts in your life? If you have never taken a "gifts" test, I encourage you to find one and take it. Not the gifts in First Timothy (pastor, teacher, etc.) but the what-you're-good-at test. Do you love to cook and have people in your home? Do you have a great sense of style? Are you great with children or teens? Are you the spread sheet queen? Whatever area you are gifted in, God created that in you! Proverbs 18:16 says that "our gifts make room for us." You won't have to bully your way in if people know you are gifted in a particular area. Now I have certainly had to wait my turn but the door always opened eventually.

When we came to pastor our church the worship team was occupied and all of the adult Sunday school classes had wonderful teachers. I felt like there wasn't room for me. But I faithfully attended a class and became a back row soprano in our choir. I should've never asked our worship pastor where the biggest need was for my voice. I am not a soprano but I falsetto'd my way through each selection for four months. When one of the worship team members left for college, our worship pastor asked me to fill her spot. I've been a soprano, alto, and tenor - all with a good attitude. I never had to push my way into a position. My gift made room for me. As for teaching, I faithfully attended Charles Smithwick's class for nearly two years before a teacher moved and left a vacancy. In that time I learned from Charles a deep appreciation for the Word that I'd never encountered. I only thought I loved the Word until I met Charles! He had a great impact on how I teach today. My class began with 7 and now we are at 70. Again, the gift made room for me. Now understand you will not always get to do everything you are gifted to do at the same time. Nor will everything you do always be your best gifts. It may simply be your abilities. I've had to do a little of everything over the years from nursery attendant to cleaning toilets. Often times where there is a need, there is not always someone to fill it especially in smaller congregations. But those are the times when a servant's heart or a selfish heart is revealed. It is in the small seemingly insignificant moments that the Lord sees who we really are. Anyone can be a superstar in the spotlight. Anyone can have a good attitude when things are perfect. The question is can you still have a worshippers heart when the faint scent of Pine-Sol is lingering on your hands as you sing? Be willing to do the stuff nobody wants to do and God will raise you up to do the stuff everybody wants to do! Finding your place is not only a vital key to surviving in the ministry, but thriving in the ministry!

CHAPTER 3

Dealing with Mean People

So I wish I could tell you that I am writing this chapter based on theory rather than experience. Unfortunately, that is not the case. I also wish I could tell you that the mean people you will encounter are all outside the church...sorry, not true.

It is truly a sad fact that some of the meanest people I've ever met have been in the church. Probably one of the reasons I feel that way is because it is so opposite of how they should be conducting themselves. When I am around the unchurched I am not surprised by cursing, gossip, anger, deceit, and selfishness. I don't expect any different from people who've not met Christ. But when those in the church display these traits, I'm taken back by it! I suppose the best way to explain how to deal with mean people is to tell you some of my stories and what the Lord taught me.

Let's First Define "The Meanies"

1. The Sour-puss.

These are the cantankerous people. You can tell who they are by their frown lines. They always find the negative side to everything. They rarely smile and when they do, it's forced. I even met a sour-puss once who literally looked as if she'd eaten a lemon. When she talked, she had one eye partially closed and her face contorted a little bit. She scared small children with her "squanch-eye". Her face looked that way even when she was happy.

Sour-puss people enjoy finding negative things. It gives them purpose. The best thing to do is smother them with kindness. When their negativity is ignored rather than being argued with, they won't change, but they'll usually get quieter. You may have to confront them if their negative words are affecting the morale of those around them. But otherwise combat them with faith-filled words and kindness.

2. The Bully.

These people are usually seeking after the weak. They won't necessarily stand up against you publicly but they constantly hurt people's feelings. You are always cleaning up their messes. They must be dealt with or they will run all over your volunteers. They are snippy and harsh. They pop off at people when they feel under pressure. They live by their emotions and not by the love described in 1 Corinthians 13. They are normally good-hearted but quick tempered. If they have a teachable spirit they will change. You must approach them with kindness but if the moment calls for it, you may have to confront them with boldness. They are usually outgoing and great leaders....when they're in a good mood. I know quite a lot about bullies because I was one. But God in His mercy sent a man named Mark Haston to call me out on it. I made a decision to repent and begin to walk in love. Although growth is a process, I've never been the same. I wasn't so much a bully at church...I was a bully at home. My children, my husband, and my dogs deserved better than the way I was treating them. So thank God for His grace. I am no longer a meanie!

3. The Passive Aggressive.

You think these people are your friends until you cross them. They manipulate with tears and underlying tension. But when you really get them mad, they explode and their stink gets everywhere! They are normally routine kind of people: square box / square hole. Thinking outside of that square box upsets them. They are also tattle-tellers because they are too sneaky to say something to someone else's face. They stir up strife and do it very quietly. They are spoiled brats. However, because they are also sensitive, the Holy Spirit deals with them through sermons, worship and other means of encountering God.

WARNING: They will come to you privately and tell you how much they've been upset with you but how they are doing OK now. They've gone to the Lord with it and everything is better...but they just wanted you to know. It may come as a surprise to you because you never knew that they were upset. Don't take it personally...they get upset with lots of people.

4. The Religious.

Ok, here's the big one. The religious meanies were the ones that Jesus dealt with on a regular basis. They are the ones who condemned Him to the cross and carried out the crucifixion. That same spirit is alive and working in the Church to this day. The religious people can be a combination of any or all of the previous people we've mentioned. They are dangerous in the body of Christ because they are the first to cause division. If you don't agree with them, or you do something that they don't agree with, they will set out to do one thing: destroy you. They are wolves in sheep's clothing. They will often be your "biggest fans" and want to be your right hand helpers when you first arrive at a place of ministry. The smaller the church, the more their voice is heard. When they leave your church (and they will if you don't leave first), it is loud and vicious. They will do their best to take people with them. They will speak against you and your ministry publicly. They will stand up (if allowed) in your business meetings to cause suspicion and strife. They know enough of the Word to be dangerous and will twist Scripture for their vain arguments. They are, as Jesus said, "a brood of vipers." And if they are not dealt with, the confusion and disunity they bring will be spiritually fatal for your church.

Please let me boast for a moment. God has given my husband, Mark, special insight into how to deal with these people. He has a rule that we live by - put out the small fires before they become raging infernos. This has worked well in our ministry. Not all small fires have been spotted soon enough, but by God's grace we have never been consumed! He takes small steps such as placing a microphone at the front of the sanctuary during business meetings. This is in accordance with our movement, the Assemblies of God. It is done this way on a state and national level. If you do not get up, come to the microphone, and state your name, you are not recognized. Also, if you are not speaking to the issue at hand, you are asked nicely to have a seat. See, he did this before there was ever a problem so it wasn't perceived as a personal attack on anyone. That's just a small example of how we choose to operate. The Word says that we are more than conquerors. We are overcomers! So why would we ever live on the defense? We are marching and moving forward on the offense! We have the ball! Don't be intimidated or afraid of the religious crowd or the influence they may have. Be wise. Operate in love. Jesus said it this way in Matthew 10:16 "Be as wise as serpents and as harmless as doves." You don't have to go around confronting people every day, but be aware of what is happening in your ministry.

My Experience

I actually have…umm, several stories of run-ins with mean people (if you've been in the ministry long, you have your stories too). I've been criticized for my hair, my clothes, my singing, my teaching, my age, my parenting and on and on and on. By criticized, I don't mean the constructive kind. I'm speaking of the demeaning, destructive, damaging kind. This has not always been done from church people. It may sometimes come from your ministry peers or even your own family. The enemy knows how to wound you.

I've had some pretty angry attackers but in recent years I experienced probably one of the most vicious unprovoked attacks ever toward me personally. Over the last 10 years I have been on a quest to diligently seek out God's purposes for my life. As I have come to recognize each one, I've taken special care to cultivate that particular calling. They are like children to me. When something goes from an idea, to a dream, to a reality it becomes a part of you. With that said, the enemy knew just where to aim. The enemy will also send attacks your way when you are physically, mentally or emotionally exhausted.

It was the Tuesday after Easter Sunday when this meeting occurred. We were completely drained. The enemy likes to attack when you're tired. It had been growing into a monster for months and we knew it. We had put out those small fires I mentioned earlier where not many people realized there was a problem. Remember, the religious crowd will not be silenced by a bucket of water. It may take a fire hose! When we realized what was happening, we prayed this prayer: "Lord, change their hearts or move them out." You must be willing to pray this prayer if you want God's best for your life, ministry or church. You can't be bound by the fear of losing numbers, money or friends.

The meeting was called under the premise of their concern for their daughter and her family. But the reality was: this couple had developed a hatred for me. Me? Sweet, precious, wonderful…me? Yep! My Sunday school class had grown from 7 to 70 and it infuriated them! They despised women in ministry. I had also lost nearly 50 pounds and this was brought up in the meeting. I was called a harlot and a Jezebel. My husband was called a heretic. They ran the gamut of vicious personal slanders and at one point I honestly thought the wife was going to come across the desk at me. The meeting ended an hour later with Mark making sure they knew to look for a new church home. Anyone in the building knew what was happening behind that office door because the couple was loud and brash. When the dust had settled, 21 people left our church. Unfortunately, many of them were young believers. They saw this couple as their mentors and if they had dared to consider coming back they were threatened. Over the last few years we've run into some of the people who left. They've apologized, but are too intimidated especially by the woman, to return to our church. You see, she employs many of them and they've been told they would lose their jobs if they came back to worship with us. They've spoken vicious words about us to anyone who would give them an audience. We have, for the most part, remained silent. They were dismissed as members and are never allowed to return under our watch! Our board and staff know the entire story and some who have come to us privately know enough to understand why they are no longer with us. The Word says to "mark those who cause division" (Romans 16:17). Thankfully to this point Mark has not had to do that from the pulpit. But if the case were extreme enough, he would. We've not been called to go around defending ourselves or tell our side of the story. Proverbs 17:28 tells us that "even a fool looks wise if he keeps his mouth shut." We are called, however, to lead, feed and protect the people to whom we've been assigned by God to serve.

I want to stop at this point and recommend - I mean highly recommend - a book to all Pastors and their wives, "*Unmasking the Spirit of Jezebel*" by John Paul Jackson. It is, in my opinion, one of the greatest tools a leader can have in the arsenal! What I have just described is, in fact, a perfect description of someone operating under the control of the Spirit of Jezebel. Trust me. You will not regret reading this book.

How to Get Over Attacks from the Meanies

There's really only ONE WAY to get over these attacks: don't take it personally. If you don't take things personally, you can avoid a great deal of hurt and offense. You may say "But it <u>was</u> a personal attack!" Believe me. I understand where you're coming from, but the truth is, it was only personal to the attacker. They think they are going after you but they are only the puppet, not the puppet master! The puppet thinks they are acting on their own accord and motives but the puppet master is actually the one in control. With the

Lord there is always freedom including having a free will. "It was for freedom that Christ set us free" (Gal. 5:1)! God does not manipulate us into doing the right thing. He places the choice before us then we act in accordance to His will or we don't. It's our choice. With the enemy there is always bondage. You think you're doing what you want but you've been manipulated into doing what he wants you to do.

My point is that when someone thinks they're attacking you they are actually attacking the Kingdom of God which you represent. Ephesians 6:12 (NLT) says, "For we are not fighting against flesh-and-blood enemies, but against evil rulers and authorities of the unseen world, against mighty powers in this dark world, and against evil spirits in the heavenly places." When you keep that in mind you recognize that it's not personal. You are simply another soldier in God's army that the enemy wants to destroy. Verses 13-18 of this same passage give us the strategy that we are to use against attacks. It doesn't say anything about going around telling your side of the story, lying in bed crying for days at a time, or allowing offense and bitterness to fester over years of rehearsing painful scenarios. It says to take up the whole armor of God, plant your feet, and STAND! I love the Scripture in 2 Chronicles 20:17 that says, "You will not need to fight in this battle. Position yourselves, stand still and see the salvation of the LORD, who is with you, O Judah and Jerusalem!' Do not fear or be dismayed; tomorrow go out against them, for the LORD is with you."

The Lord was telling them through the prophet to simply position themselves and watch the victory unfold before them. In essence he told them "Find a good view because I'm about to take your enemy out and I want you to see me do it!" Praise the Lord! This fight is not about us! It's about the

Kingdom and when someone messes with the kingdom, the King takes action!

These attacks may feel personal and may even take you a minute to gather yourself. I was almost in shock for two days after this situation occurred. When I came to my senses and got alone with God this is the Rhema word He gave to me: "Attacks are not personal, but the Favor, protection, and purpose I have for you are very personal!" I was also brought to Micah 7:8 that challenges us to say, "Do not rejoice over me, my enemy. When I fall, I will arise! And when I sit in darkness, the Lord will be a light to me!" Somebody may knock you down but they cannot knock you out unless you allow it! Get up and dust yourself off. Ask God for divine wisdom in how to deal with these people. Keep a good attitude, keep moving forward, and you will never be defeated!

CHAPTER 4

Dealing with Stupid People...Bless their Hearts

As I was writing out the chapter titles for this book I called this one "How to Deal with Stupid People." Period. Our staff wives didn't think that sounded very sweet and Christian. Also they know how much "stupid" annoys me and felt I may have some personal feelings embedded here. So since I am a learner (and try to act sweet and Christian), I listened to them and changed the title. In the South the term "bless their hearts" covers a multitude of sins. In case you haven't noticed, I'm from the South. I invite you to grab a glass of sweet tea, kick up your feet, and discover how to deal with stupid people...bless their hearts.

Ok, ok, ok! Of course I'm just being silly and making sure I still have your undivided attention! A better way to say it is "ignorant people". They mean well. They just don't know any better. That is where we come in as spiritual mentors.

Ignorance comes in two packages - "Never been taught" and "Never wanted to be taught." The first group is made up of those who would do better if they knew better. The second group is those who are often mentioned in the book of Proverbs. There they are called foolish. They don't want to be taught, because they believe they already know, well, everything and don't need to learn anything.

As a pastor's wife, stupid people are often a thorn in my flesh, but can also be my greatest reward! Simply put, when someone finally "gets it", you feel like a success. It has to be my favorite part of the ministry bar none. Seeing people not only give their hearts to Jesus Christ, but then begin to live in the abundant life that He said He came to give them in John 10:10. When they realize that they are supposed to be the head and not the tail, the lender not the borrower, above only and not beneath (Deuteronomy. 28), it's a beautiful thing! They begin to talk differently. They think with their renewed mind. They begin to speak with faith words, not fear words. This is truly one of the greatest delights of my life! What we must remember though is that it is always a process and an individual process at that. Some will begin to grow rapidly. Some will take more cultivating. And that's ok. In this chapter, I want to give you some simple guidelines for discipling believers. They don't have to be new believers. Many people are stuck in a religious rut and are still dealing with the same mess they dealt with when they became a Christian. God has given these people to your care and it is crucial that you don't crush their spirits just because they are ignorant of righteous living.

Group 1: The "Never Been Taught"

How many times have I begun to take on a new venture only to realize halfway through that I had no clue what I was doing? Countless times, I assure you. The times that those situations turned out successful for me were the times when someone was there to guide me through the process. Sometimes I was too embarrassed to ask for help but a good mentor knows when to step in and give needed guidance. Not everyone will ask for your help, but that is the mark of a good shepherdess - knowing when you're needed. There will be times when they will not want your help, but we'll discuss that later. People need to know that it's OK when they don't know everything! They need to know that you have a time of learning, and that hopefully, you are still learning. If you weren't a learner, you probably wouldn't be reading this book! So how do we help those in our care? I'm glad you asked.

1. Lead by Example.

I have made many, many mistakes in my life. None of which I am proud of. But where I have found my niche in teaching is to be transparent enough that I'm not intimidating to those listening. My husband and I try to live a life of deep character. Integrity is very important to us. We also expect it from those in leadership in our church. And if we teach it, we have to walk it out. But I am not so arrogant that I would ever stand before an audience of any size and declare that "I would never do that!" If not for the mercy and grace of a loving God, I could find myself in any sinful or devastating situation. Left on my own, I am just a hot mess! I want people to always realize that about me. I do not think I have arrived. I do not think I will ever arrive. My relationship with God and the ministry I am called to are a daily process. So when I teach or write I will always be very open about my own struggles...to a point. You have to know where the line is between openness and too much information. I want to be an example, but there are things in my life that I don't even choose to share with Mark. I'm not hiding anything, but only the Lord can handle how truly difficult, vile, & selfish we can actually be if we allow ourselves. Some things are embarrassing. Some things are very personal. If I am struggling to the point of sinning, it's important to immediately get an accountability partner. But if it's a situation where simply going to the Lord and confessing the Word can cure things, then that's what I need to do.

Here's an example: If you have a problem with someone in the church personally, it's really not the best idea to take that to the pulpit with you. I never call names in my antidotes. It's uncool to say, "Last week I got so mad at so & so, that I cussed a blue streak - but now I'm all better." Knowing you are human and hearing the details of your fleshly actions are two different things. Capeesh? When you are too open, you're handing your enemy ammunition or it may even seem to a baby believer like you are giving them a license to sin. But when it is done with wisdom, making yourself transparent is a beautiful thing.

I preach the gospel with passion. I give no room or excuse for sin and I teach personal responsibility. I often tell the classes I teach at church "Don't come to me twice with the same problem if you didn't follow through on my advice the first time." That sounds harsh, but the reality of the situation is that I have also been through some trying, traumatic and lengthy battles. Also, I won. I didn't win by rolling over and making excuses. I won through discipline and bull dog tenacity. Believe me, I have made so many mistakes it's not even funny, but that's the point. The people whose books I invest my money and time in are not novices. They have lived what they are writing about and I respect that very much. I follow some ministers that some of my colleagues snub their noses at. You know why it doesn't bother me? Because my friends don't have a clue what they are talking about, but these ministers do! They've lived it. They've been in the same trenches I am trying to get out of presently. I respect their finish! No one wants to hear a theory when they can hear experience. There are many things I have encountered in which I have no personal experience. But I choose to search the Word and other people's testimonies so that the people I am ministering to can see that there is a light at the end of that particular tunnel! If the Lord ever did it for one, he will do it for anyone!

You will find a full chapter on being a Godly example later on in this book. So I leave you with this thought for now, people just want to know that they are not alone or some kind of freak of nature! They want to be taught how to get from where they are to where they know God is taking them. Be someone's hero! Be real.

2. Never Compromise the Word.

We live in such a seeker friendly, politically correct society that it seems you can't say anything without offending 10 people. That train of thought is infecting the church of Jesus Christ like am aggressive cancer. I'll never forget teaching a series on the Lust of the Flesh and the Fruit of the Spirit. Well, I had quite a few new believers in my class and thought it was important to define the lusts of the flesh. I had personally never sat in a class that did, so I was confused myself on what "variances and emulations" meant exactly in the King James Version. It sounded so ominous, so I decided to teach about it. As I did, I realized that there was a super sweet couple who had begun attending that was living together. They were engaged but sex outside of marriage is still sin. I heard my heart pounding in my ears, but I told the truth and guess what…they came back the next week, and the next, and the next. I never called them out of course, but I unapologetically taught what the Word had to say about fornication. They are still in our church…and they are married. I can't make the

Bible fit someone's poor choices, but I can tell them that there is a way out of the mess they've made!

We must preach the Word in a way that it doesn't feel like a giant hammer over the top of our listener's ears. The Bible is not a book of rules, it's a bag of seed! When you give someone the seed, they then have the choice to plant and cultivate it or throw it out. God never intended for there to be a condemning voice in the church. It is Satan who is called the "accuser of the brethren." But we are to make sure the whole truth of the Word is presented and then allow the precious wooing of the Holy Spirit to do His work.

We recently had a woman begin attending our church who had lived a lesbian lifestyle for as long as she remembers. She said "I never knew it was wrong." You want to know how she found out? Not by attending a Gay Rights Parade and seeing "Christians" holding up signs that say, "It's Adam and Eve - not Adam and Steve!" or "turn or burn!" Nope. It was by watching Pastor Happy Caldwell teach on the Love of God during his TV program, "Arkansas Alive." She prayed the sinner's prayer with him as she watched the program and then received a booklet from Victory Television Network telling her all about her new relationship with Christ. She began to watch Christian television because she had no home church. She saw our program on a Sunday afternoon and realized it was in Hot Springs. She came and was baptized and is now a member of our church! It's simply the seed of the uncompromised Word that brings people into revelation knowledge of what this life is all about. When Christ saves someone and then His followers share the guidelines that please Him, people will want to do what they can to be close to Him.

God's Word is ALIVE! It is sharper than any two-edged sword and will cut between the flesh and the spirit of a man. It is our responsibility to give them that Word, then show them how to walk after the Spirit.

3. Be Patient.

Y'all I am ashamed, ashamed I tell you, of what I am about to type. I rededicated my life to Christ at the age of 15 and jumped into that relationship with both feet. I was an evangelist, a missionary, a singer, a preacher, whatever I needed to be at the time. I was also stupid. I was stupid with good intentions, however. I just wanted all of my friends to serve God and stop doing stupid stuff. I wanted them to know how great a relationship with God was really possible! So I was a big mouth. I'll never forget going up to a girl in our youth group at our state youth convention and telling her that if she didn't go to the altar that she would never have the chance to repent again. What a moron. I may have even said that the Lord told me to tell her. Well, He no more told me that than the man in the moon existed. I was emotional and sad that she didn't give her heart to the Lord. She was just as hard toward Him as when we arrived at the convention. I wasn't intentionally lying to her, but I let my emotions speak instead of consulting with the Holy Spirit. She didn't go to the altar by the way. She just stared at me and started crying...probably because I scared her to death. She said she just wasn't ready. I apologized to her later. Thank God she stayed in the church. That little incident could have run her away from God and the church! But God in all His mercy and patience buffered my ignorance toward her. He placed people in my life who were patient with me and who were available to mentor me. I try to remind myself of that often as I run into those who are acting out of emotion and not maturity - somebody was patient with me.

I could recall story after story of people who have come into our church who are now amazing leaders...but sure didn't start out that way. You've got to look for the gift and not the packaging. They'll come in as the most annoying, loud, brash people you've ever met and end up as your intercessory prayer leader and one of your most precious friends (I'd like to dedicate that line to my sweet friend, Terri Bland: the bull in my China Shop). They may walk in like "Debbie-Downer" so full of negativity that you can hardly stand to be around them. One day you'll see a spark in their eye and the Holy Spirit will tell you that He's raising them up as a great person of faith! It gets confusing to the natural mind. You see all the coal, but the Lord can teach you to see the diamond. Be patient and soon you'll see empty cocoons and realize you're surrounded by butterflies!

Group 2: The "Never Wanted to be Taught"

Now, this is a horse of a different color. Everyone wants to say, "Oooh, if you call someone a fool, you're in danger of hell fire!" But they are taking this passage out of context. Jesus is speaking of hatred and unforgiveness. When I talk about the fool in this section, I am referring to the foolish person you find throughout the Word but especially in Proverbs. As I've already stated, these people believe that they know more about everything than everyone. They are unteachable and have no control over their tongue. They choose to live sinful lifestyles and then point judgmental fingers at those doing the same thing. They don't believe there are consequences for their actions. They never take responsibility for anything. I like to call it the Talk-Show Generation: "Well Dr. Phil, the reason I'm an axe murderer is because my parents refused to take me to Disney World!" They will tell you as their Pastor that they want to learn from you, when they really only want to know about you. They will say that they are accountable to you, but the first time you have to correct them, they suddenly feel the "spirit" telling them to go to another church. Or even worse, they stay at yours but make sure to have awkward exchanges with you when they are obviously trying to avoid you. They will sit in service or class and cock their head when they don't like what you're saying. They'll make jokes at your expense publicly and then say "Just kidding! Don't get your feelings hurt!" The difference in these people and the religious meanies that we discussed earlier is that they usually have no following in the church. Not many people know who they are and those who do know them do not respect them. They are a distraction and a nuisance. They are often very self-appointing type people. If your church moves in the prophetic, then they have a word for someone! If your church is Word driven, they will always have the newest revelation on some obscure passage that they are positive no one else has ever read. It's pretty sad to watch, really.

They may not necessarily pose a threat to you or your ministry, but make no mistake - it's no accident that they are such a distraction. This is one of the enemy's greatest tactics. He plants these people in our lives to be at the wrong place at just the right time. I can't tell you how many times I've ended a Sunday happy but exhausted and there they are waiting at the bottom of the platform stairs. They either have a special something "from the Lord" for me, or a mild chastisement, or my favorite one: "Umm, I just need you to know that I've been really hurt at the way you've been treating me, but tonight at the altar, God really healed me. I knew you would want to know what God was doing in my life." The spirit of slap comes on me but alas, I refrain.

Mark and I have had to deal with some foolish people. Here are 5 things the Holy Spirit spoke to me about these kinds of people in our life.

- There will always be those who resist you instead of respect you

- There will always be those who treat you like a slave instead of a brother / sister

- There will always be those who try to sabotage you instead of celebrate you

- There will always be those who would rather mock you than be mentored by you

- There will always be those who would rather sell you out than sow into you

You can't fix a fool who doesn't want to be fixed. You can't argue with them because it is never ending. They believe that they are right so don't waste your breath. You will have to correct them at times. Not fun. They will usually leave…eventually, but then another one just comes to take their place. Do not waste all your energy on them. Ignore them unless necessity calls. They are easily bored and easily distracted themselves. My best advice is to study out the difference in the foolish man and the wise man in Proverbs and the Gospels. And then? Keep moving forward.

CHAPTER 5

Dealing with Trauma

In the Amplified Version of John 16:33, Jesus tells His disciples that while here on this earth they would face trials and tribulations. However, He didn't stop there! He commanded them "but be of good cheer (take courage; be confident, certain, undaunted)! For I have overcome the world. (I have deprived it of power to harm you and have conquered it for you)!"

So why do bad things happen to good people? My husband answered this question in a sermon series some years ago. Besides the obvious thought that the enemy is coming after God's people, here is what he told us:

1. There are sometimes consequences for our own actions.

Breaking natural laws can cause natural consequences. For example, when you have sex outside of God's parameters you have the possible consequence of becoming pregnant outside the bounds of marriage or contracting a sexually transmitted disease. God is not trying to punish you. But you knew when you went to bed with that person, these were the possibilities.

2. There are sometimes consequences as a result of someone else's actions.

70

These things are sometimes too difficult for me to understand. When a child has no choice about what family they are born into - and they are neglected, abused and scarred. When someone chooses to go out, get drunk, and then get behind the wheel of a car - and a loved one's life ends tragically. When a husband chooses to walk away from his family - and his wife and children are left behind to pick up the pieces alone. I have come to rest in this truth: I may not get to find all of the answers to such senseless situations, but I do know the Healer, the Mender, and the Answer.

3. We live in a fallen world.

There are germs. There are heart attacks and cancer. There are a multitude of other negative and overwhelming scenarios simply because of sin. But we have a blessed hope! Even the earth groans for the return of the Lord (Romans 8:22)!

As people of faith we must recognize that difficulties will arise from time to time. Too often we think that the day we learn to confess the Word is the same day all of our problems disappear. Religious minded people want to blame the Word of Faith movement for giving life to this wrong way of thinking. The truth is that it is religion itself that is out of balance. Religion often expects the worst and hopes for the best or it ignores reality and gives faith a bad name. True Word of Faith teachers and ministries don't teach that you won't face difficulties. They teach that there is a way out of them through the Word of God!

Micah 7:8 says, "Do not rejoice over me, my enemy; when I fall, I will arise; when I sit in darkness, The LORD will be a light to me." Proverbs 24:16 paraphrased tells us that the righteous man may fall seven times, but, baby, he will get back up! You don't have to stay wounded or paralyzed by traumatic events in your life. God is our deliverer and He has made a way of escape for everything that we face in this life!

Trauma in Your Church

Walking someone through a traumatic event in their lives can be a very difficult ability to master. Growing up in a Pastor's home, I saw many situations my parents had to deal with although they never asked for such grave responsibility. Divorces, loss of spouses, children, jobs, health are all some of the things you may face.

I will never forget my father having to preach the funerals of suicide victims or teenagers. I was especially in awe of how he handled the tragedy of one family losing two young sons within a week of one another from a rare genetic disease. Although married and living in a different city, Mark and I attended the funeral of the second son as a support to my dad. We felt the hurt of a Pastor. God gave him such a grace and anointing to minister to this precious family. It was truly supernatural.

Mark tells the story of hearing his father cry after learning of a murder/suicide that took the lives of a father and two young children in his church. My father in law had been trying to win this man to Christ but soon after he began attending church his wife made some decisions that led to this tragic turn of events. We have personally felt the pain of families in our churches losing newborn babies. We have

72

walked beside a husband who lost his young wife only hours after giving birth to a perfectly healthy daughter. Then unfortunately, trauma begets trauma. Divorces are often the result of such unexpected events. Everyone is trying to figure out the why and how of such senseless mayhem! No one teaches you this in Bible College. It is a life lesson.

Trauma doesn't have to come in the form of death. It can show up in financial crises. In this horrific economy, people are losing their homes and businesses left and right. Children are rebelling and dealing with addictions or unwanted pregnancies. These are the times that only the wisdom of the Holy Spirit can guide you into the truth you will need to say and do the right thing at the right time.

How to Help Those Who Experience Trauma

1. Love them.

You will not ever have all of the answers. They probably don't want to hear the answer. They simply need to be loved with the love of God. I couldn't explain why some dear friends of ours tithed, sowed seed, did the things the right way by trying to sell their home, yet still had to file for bankruptcy. Their home was foreclosed. Their names were in the paper and they had to explain to her boss why this was the situation. The husband had a specialized trade business that greatly depended on the housing market and construction. They knew they had made some unwise financial decisions in the past such as choosing to live at the top of their means, but they were truly doing their best to reverse those decisions. When the worst case scenario occurred, we made sure that they knew not only did we love them, but we still respected them. We were very confidential with the situation, yet defended them when anyone asked questions. They needed a win. Us loving them and not shunning them was that win. It proved that we operated in the same mercy that God operates in toward us daily. We told them the truth so that the lies of the enemy would never cause them to withhold their tithe or stop giving into the Kingdom...because that is the ONLY financial system that works! They didn't blame God or us for the situation. Instead they relied on Him and His Word to guide through uncharted waters. They are still coming out of it but live in the supernatural peace that only God can give!

I can't imagine how the parents of a newborn baby girl felt the moment they watched her take her last breath. But I know that Jesus Himself was in that room and the angels escorted that precious baby to heaven. That's all I could tell them. I could only relay that as we stood in the NICU of Arkansas Children's Hospital, the presence of God so overwhelmed me that I was suddenly and acutely aware of the angels standing guard at the head of each baby's bed. I watched as Jesus walked the room and laid His nail pierced hand on each of their heads. Why some were healed on this earth and some received the ultimate healing, I do not know. However, the knowledge that He was there, right there with them was more meaningful to them than any words of comfort or psycho-babble I could summon. All I knew was that He loved them enough to reveal His presence to us that day. Mark chose to fly home from our family vacation and minister at the funeral. He showed love by sacrificing his time. Our girls showed love by never one single moment complaining about his absence. That is what this family needed. One simple act of love will cover a multitude of ignorance about "the answers." We are simply the hands of Christ extended when we choose to walk in love.

2. Set them up to be victorious.

After all of the dust from tragedy has settled, there are lives that need to be put back together. Yes, supernatural healing is there, but we should also take the practical steps to guide people into that healing. If a couple loses a child, they need to be in counseling. The statistics for divorce after such an event are staggering! If someone has a devastating financial crisis, be sure and get them practical information and teaching about how to avoid these things in the future. Praise the Lord if a drug addict gives their heart to Christ! It is then your responsibility as a shepherd to make sure they go through counseling, rehab, Christian addiction programs, or whatever is needed. If they can't afford it, find ways of getting them there.

I've watched as hurt turned to bitterness silently and we dropped the ball. More tragedy followed because we weren't doing the proper follow up by placing them into the trust of an accountability partner. We literally cannot do it all on our own, so we must find people that we trust to walk these roads with these believers. You cannot be the only champion in someone's life if you are going to be a good pastor or pastor's wife. You must share the responsibility of mentorship with those you have already seen grow in the things of God.

I love seeing widows sitting with families in the church who reached out to them weeks after their spouse had gone to heaven. It lets us know we are doing our job - equipping the saints. We cannot leave the wounded to die. We must set them up for the victorious life we promise that they'll find in Christ!

3. Don't beat yourself up if you can't help them.

The saddest end to these tragedies is the knowledge that we did everything right, but they fall away in spite of that fact. It grieves me. I've had to learn the hard lesson that not everyone wants to be helped. Some people find fulfillment, all be it false fulfillment, in the trauma itself. Some people do not want to move on. They set up camp at the cemetery. They build their house in a graveyard surrounded by memories and blame. They prefer an open wound to a scar. The real reason, of course, is that they've chosen to doubt the Lord or blame Him for the situation. You are His representative so it is easy for them to walk away from you.

I've seen older widows years removed from the death of their husband wrap grief around them like an expensive fur. They enjoy wearing it to church and hope that someone will ask them about it. They have no plans whatsoever of taking it off and moving on with their life. They act as if they are the only woman on planet earth who had to bury her husband. The grief actually becomes their identity.

We have personally dealt with two separate situations of chemical imbalances in leadership in our churches. They were both women. They first one caught us off guard because she was an intercessory prayer leader and we'd never seen such a thing! Some of you more seasoned minister's wives are laughing at me right now. I said intercessory prayer leader and you said, "of course it was!" We were young and her 1 AM phone call startled us out of bed. She sounded as if she was locked in a closet and about to be attacked. Mark immediately went into defender mode asking her where her husband and children were and if we needed to call the police. When she laughed at him and said she was praying for his soul, he knew we were dealing with something a little different. Basically, she had chosen to take herself off of some medication she was taking and this was the result. She scolded Mark for preaching a particular series he'd just completed and we knew that this wasn't the lady we knew and loved. After the situation was resolved, she found herself in a mental health unit in a nearby hospital. When we went to see her she was mortified at all of the nonsense she had spoken to everyone. We assured her that no one ever had to know and we loved her and would help protect her reputation. One month later they were gone leaving behind a trail of accusation against us ranging from us being unloving to demanding too much of her from a ministry standpoint. Somehow, this was our fault. It hurt.

So when the same song, different verse, different church, happened a few years later, we were a bit more equipped to handle it. We understood that because of the embarrassment someone may feel from such a taboo issue they may want a scapegoat. We prepared our staff and stood ready for clean up. It happened just as we suspected, but this time we did not allow the enemy to ravage us with guilt. We knew we had manned the battle station and loved another family through a traumatic event. How they chose to respond was not our fault. Do you remember the statement I made earlier how trauma begets trauma? Well, sometimes the enemy will try to birth it in your life and ministry. Meaning their trauma will try to sow a traumatic seed into your mind, life, emotions, or relationships. For example, if you take personally things that truly have nothing to do with you, you can find yourself in a place of insecurity or fear of "failing again." Some of the worst I've seen is when a pastor or pastor's wife counsel someone having trouble in their marriage and eventually fall prey to an affair with the person they are counseling. You must take yourself out of the situation.

We've had to make a choice to turn off our emotions from a difficult counseling session when we walk into our home to spend time with our children. The fact that we are in essence leaving what we can at the office doesn't make us cold hearted. It makes us wise. We've chosen to not allow someone else's pain to set up a place of prominence in our home. Until you learn what your responsibility is and what belongs to the Lord, you will never be strong enough to carry the weight of the ministry. Obey the words of Jesus when He said "Come to me, all of you who are weary and carry heavy burdens, and I will give you rest. Take my yoke upon you. Let me teach you, because I am humble and gentle at heart, and you will find rest for your souls" (Matthew 11:28-29 NLT). Then you will always have the strength to bear the burdens for those you've been called to serve.

Personal Trauma

Maybe you have experienced one or more of the scenarios we've discussed. How have you handled things? As ministers we are often seen as superhuman or invincible. It isn't true, you know. We have pain and weaknesses just like everyone else. Some in ministry have really perpetuated this farce: "The pastor's home is absolutely perfect! No one gets sick. No one fights. Children never disobey. No one sins. There are never any financial difficulties. And all this is true because we are closer to God than any of you mortals could ever dream of being!" And those lies have cost more people their relationship with Christ than I dare estimate. What happens is that your congregants and even your own children begin to look at you more than they look at Jesus. Your rise or fall is the wave they choose to ride into heaven. Well, guess what? We make ourselves more susceptible to attacks from Satan when we set ourselves up on so high a pedestal. Why not deal with the reality of life in the parsonage so you can know how to deal with it in the church?

Pastor's daughters sometimes get pregnant out of wedlock. PK's can sometimes become addicted to drugs, alcohol, or pornography. Unfortunately, sometimes so do their parents. We can go through financial crunches and sickness. Our marriages can be shaky and even end in divorce in some cases. But when we recognize that Jesus Christ is our Savior, not just our employer, we can be free to rest in His mercy to get us through every attack hell brings to our door! If you don't know Him as Savior or Healer or Deliverer, what makes you think you can preach the very scriptures that declare Him to be all that? He is not only those things in our lives, but He is also our example.

When Jesus came to this earth, He made a very unselfish decision. He decided that He would be willing to take off His divinity and put on humanity. As Jesus walked the sacred ground of Israel and even Egypt for a short time, He walked as man. He was always and will always be fully God. But His mode of operation here was human. He depended on the Holy Spirit as much as we should. He was hungry. He became tired. He was even angry, yet He did not sin. Had He not made this pivotal choice, He could have never said, "Believe Me that I am in the Father and the Father in Me, or else believe Me for the sake of the works themselves. Most assuredly, I say to you, he who believes in Me, the works that I do he will do also; and greater works than these he will do, because I go to My Father. And whatever you ask in My name, that I will do, that the Father may be glorified in the Son" (John 14:11-13). How could He dare say we could do the same things that He did and more if He were operating in His divinity? No, Jesus was proving to us that we could access the same authority and power through which He healed the sick, raised the dead, and calmed the storms. Isn't that amazing? So when the Word says that He has been tempted just like every other man, only without sin, then we know He's already walked through what we are facing.

Look with me at a very familiar story to us all, the feeding of the 5,000. It's a story told in all four gospels, but I'll draw your attention to Matthew's account. Chapter 13 tells of Jesus' rejection at Nazareth. You see, He's just finished ministering to a multitude near the Sea of Galilee. Multitude? Yes, great crowds were gathering themselves to Him at this point in His ministry. So He leaves to go to Nazareth, His home town, to teach in the Synagogue. You understand that Jesus was a Jewish Rabbi. He was a minister. He had people in His care. But instead of appreciating and celebrating the wisdom with which Jesus taught, they scoffed at Him. They said things like, "We know His entire family - who does He think He is coming here and trying to teach us?" Having visited Israel, I can tell you that the actual size of this country is not large at all. Don't you think that they had heard of the multitudes following Him? Don't you believe that the stories of the sick being healed, the dead being raised, and the broken being mended had made their way to Nazareth? Of course they had! These are the same people who came and patronized his earthly father's carpentry business. Maybe these were men who were boys with Jesus and were His friends. No matter how we speculate, the bottom line is these were His people and they were rejecting Him. Jesus is quoted as saying, "A prophet is not without honor except in his own country and in his own house" (Matthew 13:57). Then it says that Jesus didn't do very many mighty works there because of their unbelief. How must He have felt? He's already exhausted from ministry to the multitudes. You know how you feel after Sunday services. You feel drained. When someone touches God through the anointing on your life, it takes something from you. So He's tired and now dealing with rejection.

The story continues in Matthew 14. Herod the tetrarch hears about Jesus and His ministry and says to his servants, "This must be John the Baptist raised from the dead because these powers are at work in him!" Why would he say that? Because he had just had John the Baptist, Jesus' friend and cousin, beheaded due to his lust for his wife's daughter. Jesus is not yet aware of John's death, but the disciples hear and go retrieve John's body and bury it. Verse 12 of Matthew 14 says that after they buried him, they went and told Jesus. When Jesus heard about it, He got into His boat to be alone. He needed to retreat from everyone and everything. His strength was drained. He'd ministered, been rejected, and now had lost a loved one. But very soon the people discovered where He was and followed Him on foot. That had to be a long journey. Remember Jesus had just gotten in a boat and sailed to a deserted place. These people wanted His touch so much that they walked around the sea to where He was. The Bible says that when He stepped out and saw them, He was moved with compassion for them and healed their sick. At this point it was late and the people had traveled and were hungry. The disciples urged Jesus to send them away so they could buy food for themselves in nearby villages, but Jesus said, "No - you feed them." They explained that all they had was five fish and two loaves. So Jesus took the small resource, blessed it and every person there received all they could eat!

The feeding of the 5,000 is the only miracle other than the resurrection recorded in all four Gospels. Maybe this is the case because the Father wanted us to see that even in the face of such rejection and personal anguish, Jesus was still sensitive to the Holy Spirit's prompting to minister to people. Jesus loved people! That was His passion. His own personal trauma was never cause to walk away from His purpose!

The story doesn't end there however. Just after He ministers to and feeds this multitude, He sends the disciples on across the Sea so that He could get the solitude that He still needed. You will always need to find the Secret Place. The Secret Place is where you are restored back to health, mentally, physically, emotionally and spiritually. It's where peace is found even in the middle of storms. It is quiet. There is strength in the Secret Place. There is divine revelation in the Secret Place. There is direction and joy in the Secret Place. Jesus knew the value of the Secret Place. In the account of the Garden of Gethsemane the night of Jesus' betrayal, you will remember that although He asked His disciples to stay and pray, He Himself "went a little farther..." (Matthew 26:39). In staying behind as He sent His disciples across the sea, Jesus was regaining strength in the Secret Place.

In the middle of the night Jesus decided to go check on the disciples...by walking toward them on the water! Now before you go judging the men on that boat, put yourself in their position. It had been many hours on a stormy sea since they'd seen Jesus. Also, as far as they knew, Jesus was still in the mountains praying. Why would they ever assume that the figure coming toward them in the night was their leader? Jesus knew it so He called out for them to not be afraid. Peter says, "If it's you, Lord, tell me to come to you!" Jesus simply said, "come." Peter got out of the boat, walked to Christ, looked around at the storm and immediately began to sink.

Now at this point, you may wonder what any of this has to do with trauma. My answer is simple. As a minister, you will deal with many traumatic things whether in your church or on a personal level. We have seen how Jesus has been touched by grief, exhaustion, and rejection. What we are about to discuss is one of the most painful traumas you can encounter: the act of betrayal.

I always thought Jesus was a little harsh when He answered Peter's "drowning" with "Oh you of little faith!" So I asked the Holy Spirit to explain it to me. Jesus wasn't answering his action. He was answering Peter's attitude. It was an attitude of doubt. The Cross and ascension to Heaven was no surprise to Jesus. That's what He was sent here to do. He knew when He chose those 12 men that He was choosing them for greatness! Jesus saw the potential for leadership in those around Him. He also required leadership qualities in those people. In Kingdom leadership, when you exude strength, great faith, faithfulness, etc., you don't simply receive fame and accolades; you receive more responsibility. He would leave to go back to the Father and they would stay and begin the church universal. They would continue His work through the power of the Holy Spirit. When He answered Peter's doubt by calling Him a man of little faith, He was speaking to the greatness in Peter. Peter was the only one to even attempt to get out of that boat. Only a man of great faith and phenomenal leadership abilities would dare put his foot on the stormy waters of the Sea of Galilee simply because Jesus said "come." Do you know who Jesus was speaking to when He said, "To whom much is given, much will be required?" That's right. It was Peter. Peter was a learner. Peter was bold and brash! Peter was one of Jesus' closest friends. And Peter was also a betrayer.

Certainly you have people in your life you've invested in greatly. You see the potential in them they cannot even see for themselves. So when someone you have so much invested in decides to betray you or turn their back on you in your most difficult season in life, it is a trauma that is not easily hurdled. It can turn the most trusting person into a cynical paranoid shell of who they were. This can happen with friends, staff, family members or spouses. You must decide which path to take when you encounter such a rattling situation.

What the Word Shows Us about Dealing with the Trauma of Betrayal

1. Jesus knew the difference in the hearts of His betrayers.

Not every betrayer will be Judas. Some will be like Peter and will desperately need your forgiveness, mercy, & restoration. Peter wept bitterly after betraying Jesus. Judas tried to get out of trouble by returning the money. Not everyone wants to be restored. Restoration requires accountability. Being repentant and sorry you got caught are two different things. The Angel sent word by way of the women at the tomb to tell Jesus' disciples AND Peter that He was risen. Do you see that Peter went back to the group even though he knew he had done wrong? He still saw himself as a disciple of Christ and was restored as such. Peter went on to preach the inauguration sermon of the Church in Acts chapter 2. Judas was destroyed by his own hands.

Jesus knew what was in their hearts. Peter spoke from his heart when he proclaimed that Jesus was the Christ, the Son of the living God! Then Jesus said, "Upon this rock I will build my church and the gates of hell will not prevail against it" (Matthew 16:13-20). The confession of Christ was in Peter's heart! Judas on the other hand spoke from his heart when he asked why Mary had wasted such expensive perfume by anointing Jesus with it. He didn't care about the poor. He was angry because he had been stealing money from the treasury and felt that it was money out his pocket (John 12:6)! You will need to discern who should be restored to your life and who needs to exit it. While Peter was learning, Judas was lurking. Who is learning around you? Who is lurking around you?

2. Recognize that not all betrayals or bad decisions from those under you are reflective of your leadership.

There was a "split" in Heaven and it sure wasn't due to a lack of leadership! It was rebellion and pride in the heart of Lucifer and those he influenced. Be free from the guilt of other people's ungodly choices!

We have had people in our lives that have betrayed us and hurt us deeply. When we inquired of the Lord as to what we could have done differently, He sometimes has told us "there was nothing you could have done." When rebellion, selfishness, pride, and sin are in someone's heart, they will make decisions according to the atmosphere they have created for themselves.

So then the discernment question comes to mind. We all think we should know the answers to everything that happens in life before it happens. This was true when we had a staff member who came to us only for a short time, but planted such seeds of rebellion, deceit and manipulation that it took years to uproot it all. We were speaking to my father in law about the situation and he said something I will never forget. He shared with us that it was possible that his working with us was God's way of giving this young man another chance. What if he came here and chose for once in his life to be under Godly authority? It would have affected his ministry positively for the rest of his life. Instead, he chose rebellion. He had an Absalom spirit operating in his life and he thought he could do a better job than any authority he encountered. This was not personal with us. It was evident in the jobs he had held and even his relationship with his own father. These were things we unfortunately did not discover until he was here on staff. The chaos in his life that has ensued following his time here is simply harvest for his lack of submission to authority.

When this type of a betrayal occurs, you must clean up the mess, heal the wounded and move on. You cannot dwell on the circumstances that someone else has created for themselves.

3. Understand that some people justify their betrayal because of your humanity.

No one is perfect. Mistakes will be made on your part. Will you allow them to cripple you or empower you? King David is one of the best examples of this situation that Scripture offers us. In 2 Samuel 11, the story is told of David's affair with Bathsheba. The chapter begins by saying that in the time when most kings went to war, David stayed home. He wasn't manning his post and stepped into a sinful situation. He saw Bathsheba taking an afternoon bath and asked who she was. He's told that she was the daughter of Eliam and the wife of Uriah. Well, as you know the story doesn't end well. He slept with her and she got pregnant. When her own husband wouldn't sleep with her out of a sense of allegiance to King David and his fellow soldiers during a time of war, David had him killed in battle. It was truly a dark spot on David's life and character.

Another moment I'm sure David wished he could take back was his actions or lack thereof concerning the rape of his daughter, Tamar, by her half brother, Amnon. Tamar was understandably devastated. Her brother, Absalom, was angry and took her in. King David, the Bible tells us, was very angry...and yet he did nothing about it (2 Samuel 13:21). Sometime later, Absalom took matters into his own hands and had Amnon killed.

At the point of someone's grave mistakes, seeds of disgust are often planted. People begin to despise someone they see as imperfect. Yes, I understand that we must take responsibility for our sins and mistakes. There are consequences to such actions - as there should be! But I am speaking of the instances where someone has made a mistake, repented, gone through a time of restoration and yet some people don't want to let things go because they believe they have ammunition for the future.

As I'm sure you know Absalom began a mutiny against his father's reign. But hidden in the book of 2 Samuel is a nugget of truth I have only recently come to see. Take a look at this: "Then Absalom sent for Ahithophel the Gilonite, David's counselor, from his city—from Giloh—while he offered sacrifices. And the conspiracy grew strong, for the people with Absalom continually increased in number" (2 Samuel 15:12). Absalom was recruiting people from David's advisory counsel. How could he be so brash to attempt such a thing since it could so easily expose his plans to one of David's "inner circle"? Absalom was too crafty to do such a foolish thing. Absalom knew to find those who had disloyalty growing in their hearts as well. Ahithophel wasn't just one of David's advisers. He was Bathsheba's grandfather (2 Samuel 23:34)! He was there during David's...indiscretions. And it didn't matter to him that Nathan the Prophet had confronted David and David had repented fully. Ahithophel obviously chose to remember "David the adulterer" rather than "David, the man after God's own heart."

David, the shepherd boy, the giant slayer, the Psalmist, the King, chose to receive forgiveness and restoration and move on. He knew these people felt they had a right to betray him, but David never forgot who he really was! In Psalm 51, David repents to the Lord regarding his sin. Verse 10 says, "Create in me a clean heart and renew a right spirit in me." David wasn't just sorry. David wanted a change in his character. Then in Psalm 55:22 David calls himself a righteous man and declares that the Lord will deliver him from his enemies! And the Lord did! Do not allow the betrayal of people to paralyze you. You know who you are, so act like it!

Here are 5 facts about people you have mentored who still choose to rebel or betray you:

- They see your instruction as criticism

- They see your concern as an irritation

- They see your accountability as controlling

- They see your authority as unnecessary

- They have selective memory about the positive things you've done for them

Can you be healed from trauma? Absolutely! I am a living witness. During my parents' divorce I realized that I had a very obvious choice: Stay or go. The enemy tried his best to discourage me. He whispered intimidating thoughts to me such as "If your parents couldn't make it, what makes you think you can? You're no better than they are. As a matter of fact, you were raised by them. You WILL end up like them! It's a joke if you think you're going to do any of the things you dream about doing!" You see, I come from a Spirit filled pastor's family. There are three girls. They married young and pastored for years. Sound familiar? It looked very much like the beginning of my life. The enemy knew what he was doing by tormenting me. I was very angry that my parent's marriage of nearly 32 years ended the way that it did. I was angry that my sisters and I found out on a family vacation, I was pregnant and celebrating my 30th birthday. I don't say any of these things to dishonor my parents. I truly want you to know how multi-faceted this actually was for our family. The details are too painful and private to share. The divorce was final in August of that year. My third daughter, Mackenzie, was born in December. By February I was a hot mess and my husband insisted I go to counseling. The first session the counselor asked, "On a scale of one to ten, how would you rate your anger?" I said, "twelve." Thus began a nearly one year quest to figure out if I would jump ship or man my post. When you are left without the security of the familiar you find out who you are in a deep way. I am thrilled to say that things between me and each of my parents have healed and are getting better each day. But please know that it took time and some very determined moments to see that happen.

There were Sundays I would stand at the pulpit and greet our congregation and pray to God that they couldn't see how emotionally and spiritually fragile I was. I wondered on several occasions if they knew I was considering getting in my car and never coming back. My entire belief system and heritage were shaken to the core. But at the end of all of my analyzing and speculating, Jesus was there. The One who called me assured me He still wanted me. The same Holy Spirit who would anoint me with power for service, showed Himself as Comforter. The Father truly became "Abba" to me. As I released myself fully to God and the call on my life, I fell more in love with Jesus, the Word, the Holy Spirit and with daddy God than I had ever been in my life. I received a LOVE MAKEOVER! And that caused the Fruit of the Spirit to explode in my life. This became a snowball effect in every other area: my marriage, children, friendships, and ministry! Every single place was saturated with the Glory of God! This Healing Power of Jesus Christ is still available to you! You can still be effective in ministry no matter what hell you may have faced. God is not finished with you and I pray that this chapter has caused you to decide that you are not finished with Him!

CHAPTER 6

Living Example or Sacrificial Lamb?

It's up to you...well, most of the time

Living in the glass house of the ministry can often feel like no decision you make is left unscrutinized. Oh, how often have I heard, "Is that a new dress? Why are you home schooling your girls? Do you really have time for that?" Or my personal favorite, when returning from a ministry related trip, "Did you have a good vacation?" "You guys sure are gone a lot!" Just repeating these foolish statements begins to raise my blood pressure.

I'll never forget purchasing our first home. There is no parsonage where we pastor, so we were able to choose our own home! Eighteen months after we arrived, we closed on a 1700 square foot, 3 bedroom, 2 bath nearly 40 year old ranch style home with lake access in our favorite school district in the area. One afternoon on my husband's day off, we were standing in the front yard when a man from church drove by slowly, turned around and rolled down his window. The words that came out of that man's mouth absolutely floored me. He said, with a deep southern drawl, "Well, we heard y'all bought a house. Just wanted to come by and take a look. I'll tell you this, I'm glad to see y'all are living in a normal house just like everybody else. Not like our last pastor, living in that big nice house." Mark slowly reached his arm toward me so I wouldn't charge that brand new $45,000 truck the man was driving.

The point of this story is that you will always have people in your life who choose to see you as their property. They "pay" you, so they feel they should have a say in your personal decisions. The perverted mindset that ministers should starve so they'll be humble is straight from the pit of hell. They don't believe in the honor of the ministry or the prosperity of believers (except themselves) period. They'll judge your home, your clothes, your children, your sermons, your marriage…shall I continue? You can't please these people so honestly there is no point in trying. What I want to express in this chapter is the importance of being a Godly example to those who are in your life and church for the right reasons. You may not be able to please all people, but there is no reason to go around trying to make enemies either. "Blessed are the peacemakers!" It is my sincerest desire that by reading this book, you avoid unnecessary pitfalls and see your ministry accelerated by the wisdom you gain. Here we go, ladies!

Fear vs. Faith Factor

In the chapter "Finding Your Place", we discussed the importance of knowing who you are and walking out that purpose. The main reason I believe we get stuck in a rut is the deception that fear brings into our lives. First John 4:18 tells us that there is "no fear in love." It also says that "perfect" or completed and mature love casts out all fear because fear involves torment.

Fear can affect so much of your life. It can cripple your marriage by showing up in the form of jealousy. It can create difficulty for your children if you are overbearing or overly protective. And it can creep into your ministry causing you to stifle your husband's gifts or your own gifts.

I know firsthand how fear can bully you into a place of intimidation. For many years, it was hard for me to even let my husband go on a missions trip without me. I was obsessed with talking to him to be sure he was alright. I was so frightened I couldn't even sleep if I were to attempt to stay home alone. Fear didn't just show up in such an obvious way, however. I had a mind that worried and a mouth that spoke fearful and doubting words. So every time I would get up to speak on faith there was an element of hypocrisy for me. Please understand, I am all for using wisdom and discernment. Have you ever heard the phrase "healthy fear"? I have heard it in church more times than I can count. But if the Word says that perfect love casts out ALL fear then where does healthy fear fit in? It doesn't. We are to walk in wisdom, not fear! An example would be snakes. I don't have a fear of snakes. The word says that if I happen upon one, that I will be protected (Mark 16:17-18). However, I assure you that I'm not going to play around with them. I don't know enough about them to know which ones are poisonous and which ones are not. So I just stay away from them all!

Fear is an open door to the enemy. I don't pretend to understand all of the book of Job, but there is one thing I've found. Job opened himself up to the enemy by fear. He is quoted as saying "That which I feared the most has come upon me" (Job 3:25). Fear is a powerful force. But thank God we have not been given a spirit of fear! Instead, we've been given power, love and a sound (or healthy, peace-filled) mind!

There will be plenty of moments when you have to choose faith over fear, and the people you serve will be impacted by your decision. As churches grow, so do faith issues. Should we build? Can we afford this project? Can we do this outreach? Can I face the church when under personal attack? Your people are watching. They want to see how their first lady handles the crossroad of faith and fear. Joshua and Caleb faced the same thing. They spied the land along with the others, but their report wasn't about giants. Their report was about giant grapes! You'll always have giants in the land. Make the decision to lead your people in the knowledge that the grapes are worth it! The Amplified Version of Hebrews 11:1 says, "Now FAITH is the assurance (the confirmation, the title deed) of the things [we] hope for, being the proof of things [we] do not see and the conviction of their reality [faith perceiving as real fact what is not revealed to the senses]."

Faith sees things the natural mind and eyes cannot see. It sees the situation as it is seen in heaven. It is not the hope. It is the assurance of the hope! If Jesus is calling us to be seated with Him in heavenly places, what He is in essence doing is giving us a different viewpoint than what we currently have now.

I'll never forget some years ago on a family vacation seeing helicopters fly over us as we lounged on the beach. They were Coast Guard choppers. What caught our attention was the fact that they were so close to the beach and continually swooping down just over the water. They were flying only about two buildings further down the beach from us. We enjoyed the rest of our day, but the next morning as we were leaving we noticed the front page of the local paper. A large full color picture made our hearts race! The picture was taken from that very helicopter we'd seen 24 hours earlier. It was of a school of large sharks. They were warning the people just up the beach from us to get out of the water! We could not see the danger from our vantage point, but from up above the picture was clearly seen! Faith eyes cause you to see not only the dangers you are being protected from, but also the promises that are being brought into your life! Problems seem so large when you are next to them, but take a few steps back and the full picture comes into view.

I'm going to show my age with this one, but I remember well the music video for Huey Lewis and the News' song, "Stuck with You." The couple end up on what they believe to be a deserted island, but in reality they discover they are on the other side of a resort island. Suddenly there is music, dancing, and food! That's where some of you may be. Seeing your situation through fear, while God is saying, "Trust me, daughter. Take a few more steps and you'll be blown away by what you find"! Fear torments you with thoughts and imaginations. Faith says, "Who cares what it looks like to everyone else! I can see from a heavenly viewpoint!"

How to Operate in Faith and Defeat the Spirit of Fear in Your Life

1. Know the Word.

You cannot have faith in faith and expect it to change your life. Faith is a mindset. It's a lifestyle. It's a spiritual discipline. But faith alone cannot be your source. The Word is your source. You can have faith in anything - your abilities, other people, banking systems, your employer. But when you have faith in the Word and stand firm on those promises, you will be unshakable! You cannot have faith in something you really know nothing about.

"Then Jesus said to those Jews who believed Him, "If you abide in My word, you are My disciples indeed. And you shall know the truth, and the truth shall make you free"

(John 8:31-32).

95

The word "abide" in this passage means to continue, to stay, and to not depart. Then we look at the word "know". It isn't just a memorization, but rather a deep understanding. It is the same word often used in the Bible for sexual intercourse. It means to intimately know and become one with The Word of God. What Jesus is telling these disciples is when you remain in His Word and it becomes a part of you, the truth of His Word will set you free in every area of your life! How awesome! There is absolutely nothing that can torment you when you are eating and breathing the living Word of God!

Some people get so anxious when I talk about truly knowing the Word. They feel as if the mystery of the Word is beyond their ever fully understanding it.

"But as it is written: "Eye has not seen, nor ear heard, Nor have entered into the   heart of man the things which God has prepared for those who love Him. But God   has revealed them to us through His Spirit. For the Spirit searches all things, yes,   the deep things of God. For what man knows the things of a man except the spirit of the man which is in him? Even so no one knows the things of God except the Spirit
of God." (1 Corinthians 2:9-11)

Paul is saying to get counsel from the Holy Spirit in order to fully understand the Scripture. Do not be intimidated by the enemy! He is only trying to get you to believe that the "mysteries" of God's Word are out of your reach because he knows if you ever get revelation of the Word for yourself, he is toast!

2. Watch your words.

Did you know that you will give an account for every idle word you speak? Matthew 12:36 tells us that. Don't speak all that you feel. It is a simple rule I live by. My emotions are given by God, but my flesh often hijacks them. I cannot live by how I feel so I cannot speak by how I feel. My goal is to speak what the Word says about my situation! When you speak fear, you give life to fear because we understand that Proverbs tells us that death and life are in the power of our tongue. The world and religion have caused us to shun positive confession as some sort of hooky-spooky mess. But remember when the Centurion came to Jesus? He said in Matthew 8, "You don't even have to come to my house. Speak the Word only and my servant will be healed!" That's the "Cheree'" version. You know what? He was healed. Jesus was astonished by this man's faith. He believed that the Word of God alone spoken with faith and power could change his entire situation. That's how powerful our words can be!

If you have been diagnosed with a disease or sickness please do not let the words "my cancer", "my lupus" or "my disease" come out of your mouth. Why would you take ownership of such a hellish thing? Call it what it is, but don't own it. Don't speak words of cursing over your kids like, "all these bad kids of mine", "you know how bad PK's can be", or "teenagers are so rebellious." I'm not telling you to deny your situation and act like it doesn't exist, but I am asking you to declare the Word of the Lord over it! God Himself called those things that did not exist in the natural as though they did. When you are facing sickness declare, "I am the healed of God!" When your children give you problems, declare Psalm 112:1-2 (NLT): "Praise the LORD! How joyful are those who fear the LORD and delight in obeying his commands. Their children will be successful everywhere; an entire generation of godly people will be blessed." If you face financial distress, just keep speaking Psalm 112:3-9 over your situation:

"They themselves will be wealthy, and their good deeds will last forever. Light   shines in the darkness for the godly. They are generous, compassionate, and   righteous. Good comes to those who lend money generously and conduct their   business fairly. Such people will not be overcome by evil. Those who are righteous   will be long remembered. They do not fear bad news; they confidently trust the   LORD to care for them. They are confident and fearless and can face their foes   triumphantly. They share freely and give generously to those in need. Their good   deeds will be remembered forever. They will have influence and honor."

Even some of my non-Charismatic sisters ought to be shouting for that promise! His Word works! Declare his promises, stand firm on them and wait to see the salvation of the Lord!

3. Let your actions line up with what your mouth is speaking.

Many times we speak the right thing, but walking it out is a different story. You say you want to get out of debt. You declare financial freedom scriptures over your life, but you find yourself still spending needlessly on credit cards because you're afraid you won't be able to afford something. Or maybe you need to lose weight and you are saying all the right things but never exercising or exhibiting the fruit of self control in your kitchen.

Remember faith without corresponding action is dead (James 2:20). We must put feet with our faith. It is the proof that we truly believe what we say we believe. Your testimony of being a woman of faith will have a greater impact when people are able to see that you have put into practice what you are teaching. Trials will come, but that isn't a symptom that you

98

don't have faith. No way! It's simply another moment when you can put your faith into action.

God is calling you to a deeper level of faith and I want to pray for you right now:

> Dear Father, thank you for my sisters who are sowing a seed of their precious time to read this book in order to grow as a leader. I ask you to impart to them the Gift of Faith mentioned in 1 Corinthians 12. I pray that as they apply themselves to the study of your Word, the seed of that Word would produce a great harvest in their lives. I rebuke every foul spirit of fear, intimidation, and competition in the Name of Jesus! I ask you to release warring angels over their lives to take out every principality of fear and I ask You, Holy Spirit, to invade their hearts and minds with supernatural peace. We know that faith comes by hearing and hearing comes by the Word! So may they know the Word, speak the Word and walk according to the Word!

Now, just say, "Lord, I agree with and receive this declaration by Cheree' into my life! May I never again be the same in Jesus' name!"

The Facebook Factor

I love social media! Twitter and Facebook have offered me an avenue of influence I never imagined. It makes my life easier. I make announcements to our church. I encourage people through the Word. I even act silly and post pictures of my Thanksgiving turkey. What an amazing time in history we are privileged to enjoy! The internet has done wonders for the spreading of the Gospel and communication in general. But, y'all know what I'm about to say. These people posting all their personal business on Facebook is so ridiculous I just can't put it into words. Hold your hats, ladies - mama is about to step up on her soapbox!

Now it is one thing for me to see some foolishness posted by some heathen I went to high school with or even some questionable material by a baby Christian. But when I see men and women of God posting things about fights with their spouses or not so vaguely alluding to some problem in their church, I am appalled! A staff pastor ranting about their Senior Pastor gets me every time. I just can't help thinking, "Honey child, you better be thanking God in Heaven that you are not on staff with The Reverend John Mark Haston. You would not have a good next day in the office!" What are these people thinking?

I see pastor's wives posting about how depressed or lonely they are and not even considering how it could negatively affect their ministry. And why in the world would you post some pictures of yourself in a bathroom mirror? Why would you have an album titled "Just Me ☺" if you are a grown woman?

I know we hear this often, but what you post to the internet is never truly deleted even if you can't see it anymore. I'm teaching this to my daughters. I'm very grateful that I have not had the heartache of dealing with rebellious children, but I assure you I am giving them preventative medicine. Our oldest girl learned this the hard way when she first opened a Facebook account.

I am originally from West Memphis, Arkansas and West Memphis never really gets out of your blood…then you pass it on to your children apparently. She posted a picture where she was "throwing gang signs" being silly. A man in our church posted how offensive and demonic these signs were and proceeded to embarrass her publicly. Daddy quickly stepped in to rescue his girl. He dealt with the man and I helped her delete a few people. She isn't the pastor's wife, but she was prime target for accusation over something extremely innocent and funny. On a side note: Do not email me with all of the statistics from gang related crimes because of this last story. If you're not from the dirty South, then you probably can't understand my people. It's funny and it's a joke. Just FYI. West Memphis represent!

So if a young girl posting a silly picture gets people's attention, how much more can you cause a commotion via the internet? We all want to have fun and relax but don't forget the heavy responsibility that leadership affords you. Influence is a great thing as long as you are using it with honor. Be careful not to open the door to criticism with what you are posting on Facebook and Twitter.

Quick Tips for Responsible Facebooking

1. Never be critical of people in your posts.

It is public gossip and slander. You are to be held to a higher standard than other people. If you have a problem with someone, take it to them and the Lord, not to Facebook. Even posting about public figures needs to be a well thought out decision. You have no idea who in your church voted for President Obama. When you get online and decide to tear into him personally, you're risking offending those who don't fully

101

understand your opinion; simply state the facts about policies or news articles. Don't just ignorantly begin to hurl insults.

If you have a problem with a television minister, you better be careful. How do you know someone in your church wasn't saved or discipled under the man's ministry? I always tell our congregation "Don't stretch your hand or your tongue out against God's anointed. You are causing division among the body of Christ and most of the time you don't even know what you're talking about anyway." If you don't care for a style of ministry, turn off your television. Do not risk the judgment of God by thinking you have all the facts straight. You are also sowing seeds of a critical spirit. Don't be surprised when you reap the harvest in your own congregation.

2. Delete people or do not accept friend requests from those you know are only your "friend" to gain access to your personal life.

Being friends in real life and being friends on Facebook are two separate things, although some people don't understand that. It can even be dangerous if you accept a request from someone who you don't know. I don't really want strangers seeing pictures of my children. Our staff have recently advised Mark and me to get a ministry page because we are "friends" with many people we do not personally know. I often check my followers on Twitter to be sure there are not hackers or those who mean harm to me because of my stand for the nation of Israel. If someone gets upset with you, your staff or your children for deleting them from Facebook, that person obviously had the intentions you assumed they had in the first place. Use wisdom.

3. Do not argue via the internet.

Vain arguments are not of the Lord. The Word tells us to live peaceably with all men as much as it is possible. Sometimes people just want to fight so cut them off. Last year Mark and I were viciously attacked publicly when I deleted just such a person. He is not a believer although he constantly claims to be one. You will know them by their fruit, right? I had posted something positive about a minister I follow. He tore into it on my page criticizing this man and the movement he represented. Well, I didn't want that garbage on my page. The man is entitled to his opinion but I don't want it spewed on my people. It lit a fire in him that took months to calm. He is actually still on Facebook today, as I write, criticizing a fellow pastor. This man doesn't want to learn or grow - he wants to fight. The repercussions for arguing with a fool are too overwhelming to allow him access to those under my influence. Be careful who you answer. Sometimes it's just not worth it.

4. Do not share too many personal details.

Honestly, I do not want to know how much you went to the restroom after a large lemonade from Chick-fil-A. And yes, that is from an actual post I saw by a youth pastor's wife. Gross. No one wants to know that you and your husband were intimate the night before. Crude, I know, but unfortunately it must be said. Immodest photos and stupid videos of you will be branded into the minds of the people who see them. I have lost respect for more people than I care to recall simply because of foolish things they have shamelessly posted on the internet.

Also, be careful that you don't share too many details about vacations or extended periods of time you are away from your home. It is unsafe. Many people I know "check in" at their homes in the evenings. Did you know that the innocent post you just shared with the world is linked to a maps program that can give someone turn by turn directions to your house? I don't know about you, but I really don't want to open the door for the enemy to send a fool to my property. Please think before you post. You will save yourself and your husband more grief than you can ever imagine. Oh - friend me!

Finance Factor

Preachers and money - one of the world's favorite targets. I am really bothered by the fact that hip hop moguls, the Hollywood elite, celebrities, and even politicians can live however they choose without scrutiny but let a preacher own an Escalade and news helicopters start flying overhead! This "poor preacher" mentality has been perpetuated by religion as well. It's really disgusting if you think about it. Twisted scripture, manipulated policies, and condemning "preaching" are all ingredients in this poison I call a spirit of lack or poverty.

I am also acutely aware of the wolves and deceivers who call themselves men of God when they are simply salesmen. They have given the ministry a bad name. And then there are those preachers who have an entitlement mentality and assume everyone should give to them without any accountability on where the gifts or offerings go. They expect free food, free cars, free rent, etc., just because they are "anointed by God". They have no work ethic but expect handouts. I believe this brings a reproach to the very Gospel that they preach.

So with these things in mind, let's talk about how this generation can reverse the curse that has been put on ministry and finances. The Word has much to say about money. But since many of us don't ever study out or minister from these passages, we sometimes don't know the real truth about Godly finances. I want to take some time and share a few principles with you.

How to Live in the Prosperity of God

1. Understand what true Biblical prosperity really is.

"Let those who favor my righteous cause and have pleasure in my uprightness shout   for joy and be glad and say continually, Let the Lord be magnified, Who takes
pleasure in the prosperity of His servant"

(Psalm 35:27 AMP).

The word "prosperity" in this verse is translated Shalom. Shalom is not simply "peace." It means nothing missing, nothing broken. So many ministers that I have known over the years have such a problem with the word "prosperity", and I'm very confused by this. Why wouldn't God want you to prosper? Why wouldn't the scriptures and passages concerning wealth belong to us, His children? I decided long ago that if a promise was in the Word, it could be applied to my life.

I watch churches, denominations and ministers struggle and wonder why they don't turn to the Word. Do they think this is God's will for them? Missionaries can't get to the field they are called to because churches can't give enough to send them. Retired ministers are struggling in their twilight years because no one ever taught them that it was alright if they accumulated wealth in order to live out their years in financial peace. Or worse, maybe the churches they pastored tried to starve them to keep them "holy." It's a vicious cycle that's promoted from the very pit of hell! Let me make myself very clear when I say that it is God's will that you prosper in every area of your life. If you take issue with this statement, I dare say that I could quickly get to the bottom of your perception by asking a few simple questions about your past. Most people who disagree with the prosperity message have never studied it out for themselves. They have simply taken the word of some spiritual authority in their life who was probably passing on an opinion of some authority in their life.

I have personally taken a lot of heat for my stance on this issue. Some people I know, including ministers, have never personally looked into the scripture for the truth. Unfortunately, this is true of so many people universally. When we began to need a miracle in our personal finances many years ago, we chose to go to the Word instead of our friends. Mostly because most of our friends were as broke as we were! We could see that they obviously didn't know how to get out of this mess we were all in so we needed to find the answers for ourselves. What we found has set us free. You want to be free? Stop listening to opinion and find out what the Word says.

Nothing missing, nothing broken means sickness has no right in our home. Strife has no right in our home. Demonic oppression has no right in our home. Rebellion has no right in our home. Violence has no right in our home. Perversion has no right in our home. Ignorance has no right in our home. And LACK has NO RIGHT in our home! 3 John 1:2 says, "Beloved I pray that you may prosper in all things and be in health, just as your soul prospers."

I recently heard Dr. Ron Phillips, of Abba's House in Hixson, TN, explain this scripture. He said that the word used there is not "spirit" it is "soul" which of course means your mind and your thinking. I had honestly never paid attention to that fact. I had always thought that if my spirit man was prospering (walking in love and holiness in all areas of my life), that I would prosper and be in health. That's the reason I was confused every time we came up against a financial or physical road block. But what it is really saying is that you can be doing all the right things, but thinking and operating in a wrong mindset. And a wrong mindset can block prosperity from coming to your house. You must renew your mind in the Word daily! Placing your faith on the bedrock of tradition and not truth is lethal.

God wants to bless you! He wants you to get in touch with the truth of sowing and reaping. He never intended for you to struggle all of your life. He also wants you to know why He wants to bless you. It's very simple. God blesses you so that you can be a blessing. Period. It's all about the Kingdom! A missionary calls you. You know they need to get to the field and have little time to scrape up tiny offerings and spend all the money they have on gas to go from church to church. How about instead of doing a bake sale, you simply write them a check out of your "Seed Account?" You say, "I don't have a Seed Account." Well, you could if you were living in prosperity. You would have enough to return your tithe to God, pay all your bills, take care of your family, and then have the ability to say yes to God every time He asked you to bless someone. Now does that sound evil and greedy? And here's the other part of that, it's OK if you live in a nice house and own nice things. The problem isn't owning nice things - it's the nice things owning you! God knows that every luxury item I purchase or is given to me is not a chain on my life. If He asks me to give it away, I do it. The reason I can do it with no fear is because I know He will return something to my life. He has something bigger in mind for me. I don't always get a purse for a purse. No, my harvest may be a spiritual or relational breakthrough I have needed. It may be healing in my body. It may be divine opportunities opening up in my life, but whatever it is, God promised when I release something from my hand, He will release something from His hand.

Many people think it sounds spiritual to say, "Oh, I don't give to get something from God, I just do it because it's the Christian thing to do." That doesn't sound spiritual. It sounds ignorant. By ignorant, I mean it lacks knowledge of scripture. Here's what the Word says:"Give and it will be given to you: good measure, pressed down, shaken together, and running over will be put into your bosom. For with the same measure that you use, it will be measured back to you" (Luke 6:38). That sure does sound like the Lord wants to release something into your life when you give. Are you going to live by tradition or truth? "Oh well, Cheree', that means He's preparing a little treasure in the corner of glory land." Really? Here's what the Word says: "So Jesus answered and said, Assuredly I say to you there is no one who has left house or brothers or sisters or father or mother or wife or children or lands, for My sake or the gospel's who shall not receive a hundredfold now in this time- houses and brothers and sisters and mothers and children and lands with persecutions- and in the age to come, eternal life" (Mark 10:29-30).

Jesus clearly states in this passage that you don't have to wait until heaven to live in the Blessing. He says, "now in this time...and in the age to come, eternal life." Jesus wasn't poor. Poor people don't need a treasurer. Judas was the treasurer, remember? And Judas was stealing money and the disciples didn't even notice because there wasn't just $5 in the bag. Jesus said, "Blessed are the poor in spirit for theirs is the Kingdom of Heaven" (Matthew 5:3). He also told us that the poor would always be with us and we are to take care of the poor and the widows. How are we supposed to take care of the poor if we are poor too? It just doesn't make logical sense. There is responsibility that comes with blessing. There are also persecutions that come with blessing. Can you handle both of those things? Don't be angry or critical of a minister who lives in a $10 million home if you have no idea how much money they sow and give each year. It may be that their giving is beyond your mental capacity at this point. You couldn't imagine giving away $15 million a year to missions! But they can and they do. However big your God-given dreams are will determine how much you will prosper if you receive. Do you have dreams that will take billions to see come to pass? Then ask God to bring in the resources! If it's His idea, I assure you He isn't wondering how He's going to pay for it. He must, however, have a vessel willing and able to be a good steward of His finances.

I could stay right here all day, but I feel I've said what needs to be said. Receive the prosperity and fullness of all that God has for you and you will always be empowered to see God's purposes fulfilled in your life!

2. Be a consistent, faithful tither.

How do you view tithing? Honestly ask yourself that question. I believe that is why the Word mentions a cheerful giver. Dr. Mike Murdock put my feelings into words perfectly. He said that he used to see God as the "Godfather" who would offer you protection for a 10% cut of your pay. Malachi 3:10 was an offer we couldn't refuse. If we did refuse, He'd just sick the devourer on us and we'd come running back with our protection money soon enough.

Does that ring true with any of you? I'm embarrassed to say it did with me. But when I began to see God as Abba,

Daddy, suddenly I realized He wasn't trying to get something from me at all. He was trying to get my destiny to me! He is your refuge, deliverer, mighty fortress, hiding place, and Jehovah Jireh - the God who sees and provides. We've got to stop looking at the Word as a book of rules and begin to see it as a bag of seed! Whenever I sow, I will reap a harvest. This is true of sowing obedience. He tells us in Deuteronomy 28:1-14 about the blessings of obedience:

"Now it shall come to pass, if you diligently obey the voice of the LORD your God, to observe carefully all His commandments which I command you today, that the LORD your God will set you high above all nations of the earth. And all these blessings shall come upon you and overtake you, because you obey the voice of the   LORD your God: "Blessed shall you be in the city, and blessed shall you be in the country. "Blessed shall be the fruit of your body, the produce of your ground and the increase of your herds, the increase of your cattle and the offspring of your flocks. "Blessed shall be your basket and your kneading bowl. "Blessed shall you be when you come in, and blessed shall you be when you go out. "The LORD will cause your enemies who rise against you to be defeated before your face; they shall come out against you one way and flee before you seven ways. "The LORD will command the blessing on you in your storehouses and in all to which you set your hand, and He will bless you in the land which the LORD your God is giving you. "The LORD will establish you as a holy people to Himself, just as He has sworn to you, if you keep the commandments of the LORD your God and walk in His ways. Then all   peoples of the earth shall see that you are called by the name of the LORD, and they shall be afraid of you. And the LORD will grant you plenty of goods, in the fruit of your body, in the increase of your livestock, and in the produce of your ground, in the land of which the LORD swore to your fathers to give you. The LORD will open to you His good treasure, the heavens, to give the rain to your land in its season, and to bless all the work of your hand. You shall lend to many nations, but you shall not borrow. And the LORD will make you the head and not the tail; you shall be above only, and not be beneath, if you heed the commandments of the LORD your God, which I command you today, and are careful to observe them. So you shall not turn aside from any of the words which I command you this day, to the right or the left, to go after other gods to serve them."

Look at that! The head and not the tail! Above and not beneath! The lender not the borrower! God has good things in store for those who obey His Word! But God did not create us to be robots, so we have a choice on whether or not we will obey His commands. It really just boils down to trust. What would be the reason you wouldn't pay your tithe? I don't know any Christians who say, "I just can't stand God! He's not getting any of my money!" No, that's silly, right? But I have heard well meaning believers say, "I just can't afford it this week." This includes ministers. It's crazy to believe that our attitude about stewardship won't be picked up by the people we serve. If we possess an attitude of fear and unbelief, it opens the door for the people in our church to have that same attitude. Then when the church's finances suffer and our personal finances get devoured, we are left wondering why God has abandoned us. The truth in the matter is that God will never lie. If you don't tithe, He cannot and will not rebuke the devourer for our sake, because it would be going against His Word.

When we willingly choose to step outside the boundaries of God's Word, He is not obligated to cover us. But I am so grateful that in His infinite mercy He always makes a way of escape and restoration! If you are not tithing or have gotten behind on your tithe, I implore you to take these four steps:

- Recognize your sin and ask for forgiveness

- Calculate how much you have stolen from the Lord (it's not your money)

- If it's more than you currently have (which it usually is because you have opened your life to financial attack willingly), simply ask the Lord to provide the funds

- When He does (not if), immediately pay to the Lord what belongs to Him

When we receive offering at our church, we've made it a practice to give a short sermon on why we give and call it "returning" the tithe. That 10% never belonged to you. It has always belonged to God. The offering is then our gift to Him. Choose to see the tithe as a form of worship and you will never again be resentful or fearful in your obedience to give.

3. Get out of debt and stay out of debt.

As defined in the Miriam-Webster dictionary debt is "sin, trespass; something owed: obligation; a state of owing." Even saying the word makes many of you break out in a cold sweat. Debt is bondage. It is a choke hold on your life. Money is neither evil nor good – it's simply a tool in your hands. It will also amplify what is already in your heart. Money also provides you with options. That's the truth! An often misquoted scripture is 1 Timothy 6:10. People say, "Oh, money is the root of all evil!" When it actually says the love of money is the root of all evil. Poor people can be lovers of money. That's why the lottery and credit cards are such a hot commodity. It seems to be a way to get the things you want quickly. But both are simply facades of true wealth.

There was a commercial a couple of years ago that was so revealing and true. A man was riding on a lawn mower and began to describe all that his family "has" - four bedroom home, new car, lots of "toys." Then he said, "You may ask how do I do it? I'm in debt up to my eyeballs!" Some people are so jealous of all of the stuff someone else has accumulated when in actuality that person doesn't own any of those things! The bank does! Be careful of what you assume about someone else's financial state. Please don't think that I am saying if you have a credit card you are sinning. It's just that most people cannot handle credit cards the correct way. They run them up with every intention of paying them back down but before you know it, you are drowning in a sea of unwise financial decisions. You realize you can't buy a car from a particular lot because someone in your church works there and they may find out your credit score. Worse than that is when you're not even embarrassed about a bad credit score! Your financial situation says a lot about your self discipline. Now understand something, I absolutely know that there are many people who get into financial difficulties and situations that they cannot control. I also understand how the stupid decisions you can make when you're young can hound you for years. But I'm here to tell you from experience, getting out of debt and staying out of debt is one of the wisest decisions you will ever make!

Going back to the statement, "money gives you options." If all of your actual money is going to pay off your fake money accounts, then you really don't have a choice in where you buy clothes, shop, or purchase gas. You don't have an option. You can't use a JC Penney card at Neiman Marcus. But honey, cold hard cash talks. It talks at Macy's. It talks at Wal-Mart. It talks at Home Depot. Money gives you options. I can give or I can save. I can go or I can stay. I can drive or I can fly. When you are paying your money to cards you have no options. You must pay your bills and if you don't, they'll either take what you have or put such a mark on your credit score that you won't have an option to even get more credit! It's a vicious cycle and I believe it's from the pit of hell. If the enemy can't bind us up in our former sin, he wants to stop you somehow and money is often how it does it.

Please, please, please hear me when I say that the dinner out at Chili's or a new outfit is not worth it if you cannot afford to pay for it. It is a very slippery slope that can lead you into years of torment and shame. Let every area of your life be full of the freedom that Christ died to give us, including your finances!

I want to pray for you now:

> Jesus, thank you for dying for the freedom of your people. Your Word tells us that it was for freedom that you set us free and once you have made us free, we are free indeed! First, I want to ask you to give peace to the readers of this book. There is no guilt or condemnation in you, only conviction through your precious Holy Spirit. As they ask for your forgiveness for the foolish decisions they may have made concerning their finances, including withholding the tithe, I thank you for grace and forgiveness. You never hold our sins over

us and you always show us the path to freedom. I ask
you, Holy Spirit, to enlighten their eyes when reading
the Word. May scripture concerning financial blessing
and freedom jump off the pages of their Bibles. May
you lead them to ministers who preach about
supernatural debt release and financial blessing. I
thank you for the revelation that you gave to me
concerning what you want to do for your children. Your
Word says that if a thief steals something he is required
to return it sevenfold. You spoke so clearly to my heart
that you even want to restore what was stolen through
my unwise decisions: even if I open the door to the thief,
you will still help me get my stuff back! I declare
supernatural debt release over the lives of those who
have an ear to hear and a heart willing and obedient to
your Word! May they walk in integrity and in your
character! May it be done and may they never be broke
again another day in their lives! Amen!

4. Don't be prideful.

Now, if you believe and receive what we've just talked
about, or if you are already living in complete financial
freedom, you will see the blessing of the Lord overtake your
finances. You then have another choice to make. Will you be
humble while giving God glory for all He's done, or will you
hurt those who aren't yet where you are with your pride? I
believe Proverbs 25:20 in the New Living Translation says it
best:

> "Singing cheerful songs to a person with a heavy heart
> is like taking someone's coat in the winter or pouring
> vinegar in a wound."

115

This doesn't mean you can't talk about or enjoy the blessings God brings to your life in a public way, but it does mean that you take into account who your audience is. Mark and I struggled financially in our early years of ministry. I watched every single penny I spent at the grocery store or anywhere for that matter. I had a friend who had grown up fairly wealthy and she and her husband, although young, never went through the typical scenarios many newlyweds face. One afternoon, she and I were talking. I always tried to hide that we were pretty much poor, but it wouldn't have taken a rocket scientist to look around and see what we didn't have. She made this statement, "If it costs less than $5, I don't even think about it – I just buy it." What she didn't know was that if I went over budget by $5, I would bounce every check from here to kingdom come! $5 was a big deal to me. I thought about every single dollar I spent. She had never experienced our situation, so she never thought about how that may have affected me emotionally. It was embarrassing when we couldn't go out to eat. In the beginning of our marriage, we embarrassingly had our phones shut off, our electricity shut off, and every bill collector in America calling us! Her lack of sensitivity, although innocent, taught me a powerful lesson. I am so careful to whom I tell the details of our blessings. We have never publicized how much our home is worth or how much we paid for our cars. I never talk about how much either of us make or the size of our house. I also don't hide my things from people. We have dinner parties. I drive my nice car to church and I carry name brand hand bags...but I don't post pictures of them on Facebook as soon as I get them...except my Louis Vuitton handbag. The wonderful ladies of our church purchased it for me as a 10th pastoral anniversary gift. They deserved public appreciation! Besides that exception, I just simply live my life and tell people that God wants to bless them too!

I refuse to be embarrassed of the blessing of God and the harvest that has come into our life. We know what we sowed to reap that harvest! I don't have to explain or apologize. God knows He has our bank account! It all belongs to Him! But I am also aware that there are many who are not where we are YET. I never want them to feel as if our blessings came because we are loved more or are more spiritual than they are. Nope! If God did it for Joyce Meyer or Kenneth Copeland, He will do it for all of us. And when He does it for you, never speak with arrogance. Simply give thanks.

Fashion Factor

"Oh no she is not trying to tell me how to dress!" I just heard that...

Seriously, I love that we live in a time in history when a senior pastor's wife can wear jeans on a Sunday morning...ON THE PLATFORM! (Gasp!) Some of you may not be in a place where that is appropriate and that's OK too. We still choose to dress up on Sunday mornings. I cannot imagine giving up my stilettos, y'all. Mark enjoys suits and as his wife I must say he looks pretty hot in them! But some of you are into the Ed Hardy/Affliction shirt with distressed $350 jeans thing. That's cool. We live in a resort town and our people show up in suits in the winter and shorts in the summer. You'll never walk into our sanctuary and see one particular style. There are business men, day spa owners, fitness instructors, and construction workers. We have a varied appearance. If you are in our platform ministry (choir, band, staff) we have guidelines for dress simply because of television and visual continuity. Our choir chunked the robes several years ago and opted for the coordinating colors scene. We wear pants and dressy jeans but no athletic shoes. Our staff pastors still wear suits and ties in our morning services. It's all preference really. That is not what this chapter is about, however. This is about how you present yourself to those in your community and congregation.

I'll never forget finding out I was pregnant with our first daughter. It's like when I saw those two lines on that stick all my fashion sense went out the window. Now let me clarify: this was 1996 and maternity clothes had not yet evolved. We were barely out of the moo-moo stage! Giant bibs on sailor dresses were still happening. As a matter of fact, I owned and proudly wore a denim sunflower printed maternity dress. The shoes I paired with it? Oh, clogs of course! I also enjoyed wearing my denim bubble suit that was shorts, not pants. I wore that coupled with my white Keds and fold down socks. You are picturing it now. But the kicker was when I decided that a mommy needed a mommy haircut. So I drove myself to the salon where I proceeded to cut my long flowing raven hair into an Oprah Winfrey inspired mullet. Yes, I am a white lady. I just can't explain it so please don't ask. These were also the days prior to my discovering the beautiful art of eyebrow waxing. I was in essence, a hot mess. I tell you this story to expose some of your intentions. Maybe you think that because you're a pastor's wife you need to dress like your grandmother. Or maybe you have rocketed the other direction and dress in such a way that no one would ever suspect you being in the ministry! The lesson I learned was that modesty and fashion can coexist, and I need to just be myself.

I mentioned in the mean people chapter that I had been attacked by the religious meanies concerning my clothes. I had gone from a size 14 to a size 6 and this woman did not like it one bit. When I was a 14, I wore clothes to cover my flaws. When I lost nearly 50 pounds I didn't think it was inappropriate to wear clothes that fit my new figure. I grew up a preacher's kid. My parents were very good about allowing my sisters and me to wear trendy, age appropriate clothing. They never tried to suffocate us when it came to fashion, but they didn't allow immodest clothing either. There was a good balance in our home. We wore bikinis on our family vacations but not on youth outings. So with that as my history, I think I have a pretty good handle on what is appropriate and what is not appropriate church wear. This woman didn't agree with me. She tore into me about it so I asked her what she thought was appropriate. She was a sixty-something, overweight woman and pointed to herself and her...umm, outfit. It was a polyester pant suit type of thing with extremely protective shoulder pads. Its color resembled baby poop meets cornbread dressing. So I started laughing. I wasn't being disrespectful. I seriously thought she was joking! I was 32 years old and fit. What in the entire world made her view herself as a fashion example? Well, she didn't view herself as a fashion icon. She viewed herself as holier than me. Now we had a problem. I was not going to be able to please her and you will find those people in your world as well. She is not the only one to ever criticize my apparel, but I haven't allowed that to alter my perception of myself.

Some Practical Guidelines in Fashion

1. Stop trying to bring sexy back...to the house of God.

When we were pastoring our first church in Blytheville, Arkansas, there was a precious saint named Lucille Gentry. She went to heaven while we were still her pastors and Mark had the privilege of officiating her funeral. While she was alive, she became my go-to lady. You know the passage in Titus 2:4-6 that says the older women should train the younger women to live righteously and behave righteously? Sister Gentry did just

119

that. She was a humble and Godly example of a woman of God. Well, one Wednesday evening I decided to wear a skirt I had never worn to church before. It was considered a mini-skirt but still modest enough for me to wear. But when I paired it with a tall sandal, I suddenly became aware of its mini-ness. The first thing I did when I got to church was to call Sister Gentry into the nursery and ask her what she thought of the length of my skirt. With the kindness of Jesus, she looked into my eyes and said, "Sister Haston, if you called me into this room to ask me that question, then you must feel insecure in that skirt. I think you have beautiful legs but if you are going to be distracted by what others may think then why don't you wear something else next time. I want you to feel good about yourself." I asked her if she thought I should go home and change. She said, "No way! Show off your legs tonight!" She calmed my nerves for that service but she taught me to trust the Holy Spirit to guide me in what I wear.

Some of you are trusting in yourself and that isn't good. You need to ask the Holy Spirit to be present in every decision you make including your appearance. I don't want to be a distraction to the people in my church by looking like a skank in the sanctuary! I refuse to list the clothing items that I deem inappropriate for church because many things in this day and time all depend on how you wear something not necessarily what you wear.

Now there are some things that are a given. Don't wear those little cheerleader shorts or a bikini in front of your youth group! There are boys with hormones and girls with sexual identity issues and you will be a stumbling block to both just because you think you look cute! Don't wear tight shirts that outline your lady lumps without an outer shirt, sweater or jacket no matter how fantastic your new bra may be. Don't jump up and down during fast songs if you have a large breast size and a cheap bra. Some things are just common sense. My goal at church time is not to be sexy. If you are getting dressed with the thought, "I hope all the men at church see how blessed my husband is to have me." Then you are dressing with the motive to draw attention to yourself. That is wrong. I'm not asking you to wear a burlap sack in order to keep men from lusting after you. I certainly don't dress that way. But I am asking you to consider who may be watching you. We have a group of about 50 Teen Challenge men who attend our church four months out of the year. They sit right behind our staff wives. Each lady knows when it's time for TC to be there, so we need to be even more careful than usual since they are seeing us from behind. They have many addiction issues and most have been away from their wives for several months. We want them to be able to focus on the Word and God's presence without distractions.

The bottom line is this: You can be beautiful, trendy, age appropriate, weight appropriate, cute, and sassy without being sensual. If you are still confused about what to wear, find someone you trust and respect and allow them to speak into your life. You'll never regret being teachable in all areas of your ministry!

2. Wash, dry, iron, repeat.

It's a bit sad that I actually have to put this section in the book. You would think that most women would enjoy wearing clean, freshly ironed clothes and showering everyday but sadly that's not the case. When you are in the public eye you are up against pressure to look and act the part. Many people want to rebel and say things like, "He's called to the ministry. I'm just called to him." Wrong, sister. When God calls a man, do you think He is surprised when the man marries and has children? God has known us from the foundations of the world. He set our destinies in motion before we were ever born! When a man is called, so is his entire family. I've already expressed my beliefs on protecting your privacy and your children from religious minded people who think they own you. So I hope you hear my heart in this matter. Our girls know that there are certain things that we are more scrutinized on than other families, but they also know what an honor it is to be called! With that calling comes responsibility. Our appearance and the appearance and cleanliness of our home and car are all part of this life we live.

Our youngest daughter, Mackenzie, takes showers alone now. I check to make sure she is washing and rinsing everything the right way, but recently I missed it. She had gotten in trouble and was sent to the shower and bedtime early for throwing a dress shoe at her older sister's face (I'm just keepin' it real, y'all). When I woke her up for school the next morning, I rubbed her hair and pulled back greasy fingers! Then I smelled the most glorious smell: lavender. The child had washed her thin, little girl hair with my new lotion infused body wash. Well, it was too late to take another shower so I wrote her teacher a note explaining the grease and gave that baby a slicked back ponytail. I personally washed her hair the next night, but the junk still didn't fully wash out. I discovered that detail on the next morning! We did a quick rewash & dry...STILL GREASY! Another ponytail day! I know it sounds crazy but people know who we are and they know Mackenzie. If I sent her to school with dirty hair and dirty clothes and I drove a dirty car, do you really think that people would respect me as a mother?

Mark and I were financially strapped in our early years, but that wasn't the first experience of lack in my life. I was on the free lunch program in kindergarten and it didn't get much better over the years. We didn't always have a lot and certainly didn't own many expensive things, but my mother kept us clean and put together, even in our hand-me-down clothes. Most people had no idea that we were so broke because of my parents' attitude of excellence. They were always good stewards of the things they had and that included their children. My mom and dad looked like a million bucks at church and not just because my dad ironed a crease in his jeans! HA! I still laugh about that because now he sends them to the cleaners to get creased. That joker is not playing! Excuse me that I got distracted…back to the book. My mother rolled our hair in sponge rollers every Saturday night and when our patent leather shoes from Payless got scuffs on them, she discovered that fingernail polish remover would clean those dress shoes right up! Mom kept our home smelling like Pine Sol, candles, and crock pot food. She was a homemaker. She made our home the wonderful place that is was for us. I have chosen to do the same thing. I haven't always been as obsessive compulsive as I am now, but even back then in my "messy days", our house was spotless before we had people over. My present attitude of excellence has come with age and experience, but you don't have to wait on it. You can begin right now!

When your home and family are well taken care of you feel such a sense of accomplishment and relief. It relaxes you. I can enjoy my husband's day off along with him because I don't have a million things, including guilt, hanging over my head. Putting stain remover on our clothes as soon as possible keeps them nice and saves us money. I knew a ministry family who were complete slobs. They were lazy and foolish. One example of their lifestyle was that they rarely washed their clothes. They would simply go buy more, which of course they couldn't afford, so they were in a terrible financial mess. The mother of the wife would come to visit simply so she could help clean her daughter's house! Neither one of the couple really worked too much so they certainly could have done it on their own. The woman's mother would find piles and piles of her grandchildren's clothing all over the house. Most of the time, the clothing had been left there so long that they were covered with mildew and stains. It frustrated her to no end, yet instead of teaching her daughter to do better, she enabled this lazy, slothful attitude by going and buying more of whatever they had ruined.

Now I know that this is an extreme story, but except by the grace of God and wonderful examples in my life, I could have been slanted in that direction. I don't ever want to be that woman, and I don't want you to be her either. Whatever is happening in the natural is a reflection of a deeper spiritual issue. The Word says that we will be known by our fruit. Self-discipline is a fruit of the spirit. Proverbs has much to say about diligence and work ethic. You are showing your true colors by what you choose to display in public. Now I am not saying that everyone that appears to have all their stuff together really does. The fruit I am talking about is an attitude of discipline and excellence. When you see someone constantly doing a job half way, there is a problem no matter how they are dressed. I am telling you that a hidden issue will eventually make its way to the surface. If you are asking the Lord to bless you with a particular harvest, He must see and know that you are a good steward of all that He has presently put into your hand. You may have already read that a time or two throughout this book…it's really indicative of the Proverbs 31 woman.

Proverbs 31 is not an unreachable place. Verses 10 through 31 (NLT) is a clarion call for true women of God to answer. I'm going to give you the "Cheree' Haston Southern Woman Interpretation:"

Verses 10-12:

"Who can find a virtuous and capable wife? She is more precious than rubies. Her husband can trust her, and she will greatly enrich his life. She brings him good, not harm, all the days of her life."

> A good wife has more worth than precious jewels. Her husband doesn't have to worry if she will act a fool at the women's meetings, church service, or at Wal-mart and embarrass him. He trusts her not to have an affair or look to other men for self worth. He doesn't worry that she's going to cost him his ministry because she knows how to conduct herself around other people.

Verses 13-15:

"She finds wool and flax and busily spins it. She is like a merchant's ship, bringing her food from afar. She gets up before dawn to prepare breakfast for her household and plan the day's work for her servant girls."

> She is a self starter. She makes sure that there are groceries in the pantry and she gets up early to make her "to do" lists. This keeps the house running smoothly.

Verses 16-18:

"She goes to inspect a field and buys it; with her earnings she plants a vineyard. She is energetic and strong, a hard worker. She makes sure her dealings are profitable; her lamp burns late into the night."

> Sometimes she may have to work outside the home. She is smart with the money she earns. She takes care of herself physically. She works out and strengthens her body. Another way to say this is a quote from a 1980's commercial: "She can bring home the bacon, fry it up in a pan and never ever let him forget he's a man, cause she's a woman." Alright now!

Verses 19-21:

"Her hands are busy spinning thread, her fingers twisting fiber. She extends a helping hand to the poor and opens her arms to the needy. She has no fear of winter for her household, for everyone has warm clothes."

> She gives to other people while still taking care of her family. She does not send her kids to school without a coat! She switches out the winter and summer clothes in a timely manner even though it's a headache, so her kids don't go to school wearing flip flops in the snow. Then whatever they've outgrown, she bags it up and gives it to needy families.

Verses 22-24:

"She makes her own bedspreads. She dresses in fine linen and purple gowns. Her husband is well known at the city gates, where he sits with the other civic leaders. She makes belted linen garments and sashes to sell to the merchants."

> I would like to say, I have never made a bedspread. But I think it would be appropriate to say: she jets out to *Bed, Bath and Beyond* and picks out super cute comforters and duvets! She decorates and takes care of her home. Her husband is

respected because his wife is honorable. She is creative. And she looks good herself!

Verses 25-27:

"She is clothed with strength and dignity, and she laughs without fear of the future. When she speaks, her words are wise, and she gives instructions with kindness. She carefully watches everything in her household and suffers nothing from laziness."

> She is not a worrier. She is not fearful. She likes to have a good time. She is classy and strong. She tells her kids to act right, but she isn't bossy, brash or rude. She doesn't yell at her family (even when she's on her period). She keeps up with the house and calls the repairman if it's needed so nothing gets out of hand. She is not lazy. She is diligent.

Verses 28-29:

"Her children stand and bless her. Her husband praises her: There are many virtuous and capable women in the world, but you surpass them all!"

> Her kids say she is their "SHERO" and her husband brags on her to her face and behind her back. He says, "Girl, there ain't nobody in the world like you! You make big papa proud! Come over here and give me some sugar..."

Verses 30-31:

"Charm is deceptive, and beauty does not last; but a woman who fears the LORD will be greatly praised. Reward her for all she has done. Let her deeds publicly declare her praise."

> She doesn't just look good on the outside, but she is truly a woman of integrity and character. She loves the Lord and wants to please Him more than anyone else. She deserves to be honored because she's earned it!

Never one time does this passage say that this woman is perfect and flawless. It says she gets up and does these things. She chooses to be the best she can be and we can make that same choice. I want to be a godly example in everything I do from my prayer life to my chocolate chip pecan pie! I'm raising three women in my house so the pressure is on, but I'm so glad I have the Word of God and the power of the Holy Spirit to cause me to be victorious every day!

Farewell Factor

Cue the Boyz II Men song…"It's so hard to say goodbye, to yesterday-hay."

I hate goodbyes. In the ministry, you will experience more than your fair share. This job has many perks, but this is one of the few downsides. You will say goodbye to family if the Lord calls you to an assignment far from your hometown. You will say goodbye to staff members as they follow the leading of the Lord for their ministries. You will say goodbye to people who will leave your church whether by moving away or deciding to worship elsewhere. You will say goodbye at funerals of precious saints. Goodbyes are usually not easy. I suppose it depends on the circumstance. We are created to need and live in "community." Your church members will become like family to you, as will your staff. What I want to talk to you about in this section is the goodbye that comes with your resignation from your ministry position.

I've already made my feelings clear on unnecessary drama, but when you make the decision to leave a place of ministry, it can be quite emotional. Maybe you are leaving a place that you love and people that you love. Maybe you've raised your children in a church and now you must go. Maybe you are leaving a place that you despise and you've begged God since the moment you arrived to either move you or send Jesus back to take us all to heaven! It could be a place with amazing memories or a place of pain and torment. Whatever the scenario, as people of God, we must learn the art of goodbye.

I can remember the resignation services I attended as a child. I remember the tears and the secretive nature of our family discussions. It wasn't that my dad was trying to be sneaky, he was simply trying to protect the atmosphere of the worship service and the emotions of our people. I've experienced this three times in my marriage and personal ministry. We resigned from our youth pastorate 2½ years after taking the position. In that time, we had gotten married, had a baby and seen our youth group grow from 7 to 70 students. We had many students who were from rough families that we'd begun to pick up on our bus route. Every Tuesday afternoon, we would canvas neighborhoods and knock on doors in hopes that a teenager resided there. We taught our "church kids" a love for outreach and an understanding of breaking down walls of racism and prejudice. We took those kids on two trips to Walt Disney World (an 18 hour drive in a church bus) and were able to witness many of them putting their toes into the ocean for the first time. When we told those students that we would no longer be their youth pastors, it was so emotional that I feel tears coming to my eyes as I type this paragraph. We were the only stable adults that some of them had ever known. For the others, there was simply a great bond that had formed as the spiritual leader in their life.

These circumstances were magnified when we resigned from being the senior pastor of our first church. Julie, our oldest, was a month old when we moved into the parsonage, she was in kindergarten when we left. Riley, our second daughter, was born while we were pastors there. Oh…that Sunday in September…I'll never forget it. I could barely contain my emotions as we went through the motions of the service. Only our official board and staff knew what was coming. We had seen a 20 year debt paid off on the building and an atmosphere of worship was birthed during our tenure. The church had also experienced some growth, so we were leaving on a "high". As Mark approached the point in his message where I knew he would tell the people of our intentions, I braced myself. I stared at the floor as hot tears began to drip down my face. When the actual words came out of his mouth, there was an audible gasp across the sanctuary. These people loved us, and we loved them. It was difficult but we knew our season there had come to a close.

Then our most recent resignation after ten years of a very successful senior pastorate has by far been our most difficult to date. Giving our heart, soul, spirit, and sweat to a wonderful group of people who we lived life with for so long was a good-bye like no other we've ever known. Add to the mix, three daughters in school, two of which are teenagers, and moving to a place where we literally knew no one, was our biggest leap of faith…but I must add, has been our greatest time of reward!

I wish I could tell you that we did everything right in all of those resignations. I wish I could tell you that we've always done everything right, but it's just not true. But we did learn from those mistakes. I want to give you some things to remember as you follow the direction and voice of the Lord in your ministry.

How to Say Goodbye with Grace

1. Proceed with caution.

With any assignment the Lord gives you, He also provides the grace to do the job with your whole heart. Suppose you go to a ministry position in the inner city. You know the Lord has placed you there because you have a heart for the people, and a passion for the assignment. But when your family comes to visit, they may see your "promised land" a little differently than you. You see the vision - they see the obstacles. Make sense? It's the same way when you visit another church or town and say "thank God we do not pastor here!" But the people who are assigned there love the place! So just as that grace comes on your life as you enter an assignment, it will lift as you exit. And I will tell you, the grace always lifts before you actually leave. This is all part of the process of discerning the will of God. When you sense the grace lifting, you will begin to ask questions of the Lord. Grace will always lift before change occurs. Sometimes that change is a staff person leaving or a shift in your own ministry and it will not necessarily be a physical move for you personally. Only you and the Lord can determine what and when the change should be, but if you are a person who spends time with God, you will know His voice.

The reason for the heading "proceed with caution" is simply that you must search out the true reason for the lifting of the grace. If you don't, you may make some fatal mistakes. When grace lifts, there are some common side effects. There will be things that never bothered you about people, places, and things that will begin to get under your skin. The pastors, staff and leaders, that you work with will begin to annoy you. Their mistakes are magnified, their quirks are magnified and their differences from you are magnified. You must be careful not to react out of your flesh. And you must remember that they probably have not changed - you have changed. This is of greatest importance during the waiting period between your realization that God is moving you to the "when and where" God is moving you.

Another characteristic of lifted grace is anxiousness and impatience. Mark and I fell prey to this at our first church. We had talked to a couple of boards at churches in different cities, but did not have a peace about taking the pastorate at these particular places. So we decided to do what any good man and woman of God would do, step out in faith. We told the Lord that we did not want to hurt the church we were pastoring by overstaying and we made the decision to resign before we had another position. I'd like to add, we made the wrong decision to leave too early. Our reasoning sounded so spiritual and selfless, but now years removed, we can see that we were in essence trying to manipulate God with our great sacrifice. The church was fine. They elected the man that Mark recommended with a 100% vote. We, on the other hand, were both working secular jobs and preaching / singing at various places on the weekends. We felt like we'd fallen off the edge of the earth. Our "great friends" who were pastors barely called to check on us, I suppose because they were afraid that we would ask for a service. Maybe some of them thought that we would go after their church – who knows. We couldn't make ends meet financially and were struggling with our identity as ministers. It was a dark time. I'll never forget the Christmas season we spent out of the pulpit as Mark and I were walking around Sam's Club in Little Rock, Arkansas. We couldn't really afford anything but it gave us something to do. I was doing alright until I came to the paper goods aisle. When I saw those giant packages of paper plates and Styrofoam cups, I lost it. Why? It reminded me of all the church Christmas parties that were happening all across the world…and we, for the first time in our lives, would not attend one. It was a strange moment. Our time out of full-time ministry lasted for 7 months. It felt like the back side of the desert, but God was so merciful to us and brought to where we are still pastoring today!

Proceed with caution in every decision that you make. Choose carefully who to confide in about your feelings. Don't get ahead of God. You don't want to create an "Ishmael" when God is simply asking you to wait for "Isaac."

2. Don't take things personally.

I understand that we have covered this subject more than once, but it is important to understand the reactions people will have when you announce your departure. There will, I repeat, there will be people who take your resignation so personally offensive that they might not even return to church until after you have left. Even if you are leaving in a very positive way, they will feel rejected and hurt. You could be taking a huge promotion, naturally speaking: a larger church, larger salary, and larger city, but they will only feel rejection. You have to be able to handle that correctly or you will do more damage than good. I did a stupid thing (shocking, I know) toward a staff person as we left our pastorate. She decided to change a baby shower date that I had set and it just infuriated me. I shot off at the mouth in front of our church people and looked like a jerk face idiot. Truthfully, she did overstep her bounds. It was too soon to be making those kind of decisions right in front of me as I was still reeling from the sadness of saying goodbye to people. Staff wives take note: it was a simple change that she had every right to do after we were gone. As a staff wife, no matter how long you've been at a church, you cannot fully put yourself in the shoes of a lead pastor's wife. We are in much deeper than you realize. My insecurities about who would take my place were already front and center, so this announcement she made both in front of me and a group of our women was just more than my flesh could handle that night. We had people who we considered dear friends in the church who decided to tell us all of the things that we had done wrong as their pastors over the 5 years we served them. It was just out of nowhere and it hurt. We were not prepared for some of the reactions that we received. But thankfully, there were also some who responded in great honor, love and respect for us and the call on our lives. They told us that they were proud of us and knew God would take us big places. We made a choice to focus on those people and the positive memories we had from our time at that great church. I hope that you will choose to focus on the same.

3. Don't be a jerk.

Don't be a jerk even if they have been jerks to your family. Jesus told us to love our enemies and to turn the other cheek. You are obviously not being their doormat if you are leaving, but it's really not necessary to tell them all of your feelings toward them, their mama, their bratty kids, and their stinky town. If you are a staff person, you have no right to dishonor the pastor that you have been serving even if he is a dishonorable person. Remember, David and Saul. There is just no reason to leave on a sour note if at all possible. Do your best to not burn bridges. This is the Kingdom of God we are talking about and in this Kingdom, the Prince of Peace still reigns. Act like you belong to Him. He will reward you for exhibiting the fruit of the spirit when you really just want to exhibit the spirit of slap! Pastor's wives, honor your staff when they leave with a dinner or goodbye party...unless they have been rebellious and stirring up strife. In that case, don't even let them stay 2 weeks. Hand them a severance check and tell them to hit the road (in love, of course). The other side to being a jerk is bragging about and talking too much about where you are going. That can hurt your people. They may be very happy for where the Lord is leading you and excited about promotion in your life, but they do not want to hear all about how excited you are. Translated in their minds - how excited you are to leave them. Consider the feelings of those who have supported and loved you during your season with them. Goodbyes can be difficult, but with godly wisdom, you can make the transition for you, your family, and your church a smooth one covered by the peace of Almighty God.

Chapter 7

The Diva Syndrome: We've Been Called to Serve

Diva. Just the word conjures up pictures in our minds of diamonds, animal print and high heels. I have the sudden urge to watch an episode of "The Real Housewives of..." Well, not really. These days you can purchase T-shirts, hats, throw pillows, coozies, tank tops...shall I continue? An unlimited list of items with the word "DIVA" splashed across them with blingy rhinestones!

I used to call myself a diva thinking I was being cute. But then I found out what a true diva actually is: a prima donna, a woman who will do anything to get what she wants. In Italian, it is literally translated as a female god. Beyonce' even says that a diva is a female version of a hustler...so there's that. Truthfully, I don't want to be any of those things. I don't like people like that. They manipulate situations to get what they want. That just doesn't sound very godly. "Kingdom Divas" (a term I have created for this chapter) are those who walk around like Jesus is lucky to know them. It's disgusting.

Last year we were discussing possible events for this year and one idea was to have a women's conference here at the church. We are involved in several others but tossed around the idea of hosting one. I was put in charge of calling some ministries (which shall remain nameless) to check out the costs and other details of having them come to our city. We wanted a "big name" for the draw. I received a return call from one ministry quickly. They had a list of suggestions and what they normally expected to receive as far as an offering, travel expenses and accommodations. It was over budget for us but the lady who I spoke with was sincerely willing to work with us on any of their normal "demands". She was a sweetheart and very humble. The second ministry didn't call at all. As a matter of fact they emailed our secretary a list of expectations and a contract to sign and return along with a very large deposit. The cost to bring this "minister" into our city was an unbelievable $38,000 for one service which would include four songs. There was also a list of meals that would have to be provided. This was not a suggestion. It was an actual menu. They also required a particular type of car and made it clear that anything else would be unacceptable. She would only be bringing in 5-7 people, so we only had to get 5-7 rooms at a five star hotel. I trust you sense my sarcasm.

I believe that a workman is worthy of her hire! Do not bring someone to your church who is in pretty big demand and give them $100 and a potluck dinner. If you can't do something with excellence then you need to wait until you are able. But this celebrity mentality that is so prevalent in our society has leaked its way into the church!

The first ministry I made contact with is absolutely on my list of future guests and we will give her what she requests. There was such a humility and kindness in the attitude of her staff. I have been in meetings with this woman and she is anointed of God! But the second ministry? Ahahahaaaaa!!!! I still laugh about that contract. If you want to be a celebrity, be a celebrity. I am not judging her for that. But if you call yourself a minister, there must be an attitude of servant hood.

Now that we've been around a few years, I watch to see how other ministers interact at our movement's state and national meetings. We also attend a Word of Faith ministers' conference each year and see how people who have no clue who we are treat us there. It's very interesting. Some people are so kind it catches me off guard! But the insecurities of some make them appear to be rude and arrogant. And then there are those who really do think they are a gift to everyone around them and make sure everyone "appreciates" them as such. People prance around and demand to be treated a particular way but choose to overlook everyone in their sphere of influence. This attitude can be found in both movements. There is an air of entitlement that I believe grieves the heart of God. I refuse to have a conversation with someone who looks past my head to see if there is someone more notable behind me. I have been known to stop in mid sentence and say "Well, it was nice seeing you." And just walk away. The crazy thing is that they normally don't even realize I stopped my story halfway through.

Mark was the president of his Campus Missions Fellowship during his senior year at Central Bible College. One of his responsibilities was inviting and hosting speakers for their Friday night service. He has often said that the higher the office the person held who came to speak, the more humble the person was. This wasn't always the case of course but it was the general feeling. He said it was the men who were "on their way up" who normally treated him like a "nobody college student". They were sometimes rude and simply wanted him to be their "connection" to the President's office. They had no use for him. He was often shocked, however, when the men of higher position would sit and ask him to tell them about himself and his vision for ministry. They wanted to know where he felt the Lord was leading him and what his ministry dreams were. Those encounters made an impact on how we now choose to do ministry. See, it's the "nobodies" that could be the key to your destiny. It was a small boy whose lunch fed the 5000, it was a lame man who entered the Temple walking and leaping and praising God & telling about the power of Peter and John's ministry! It was an unlikely person in our lives, Kandi Rose, a Jesus-loving former stripper and former drug user who introduced us to the people who opened the door that began our TV ministry. Kandi wasn't a "nobody" to us, but she wasn't someone who would've appeared to have had the contacts she had made in her life. We just simply loved her because we were her pastors and adored her zeal for our Lord. The Favor of God did the rest!

Jesus had every right to come to earth make all sorts of demands for His "Evangelical Association." After all, He was the literal Son of God. Instead, He made it very clear in Matthew 20:2-28 in The Message:

"When the ten others heard about this, they lost their tempers, thoroughly disgusted with the two brothers. So Jesus got them together to settle things down. He said, "You've observed how godless rulers throw their weight around, how quickly a little power goes to their heads. It's not going to be that way with you. Whoever wants to be great must become a servant. Whoever wants to be first among you must be your slave. That is what the Son of Man has done: He came to serve, not be served—and then to give away his life in exchange for the many who are held hostage."

The disciples were hot when they heard what James and John's mama was up to! When you try to elevate yourself, you will only alienate yourself. Jesus wasn't going to play into the mentality of "earthly kingdom." He knew what His purpose was here and what He had to do to accomplish it. Satan had already tried to go after Christ's pride in the wilderness. He told Him that he would give Jesus all the earthly kingdoms and glory if He would just compromise who He (Jesus) was and bow down to Satan. Jesus rebuked Satan and told him to go as He quoted the Word! That is what we have to do when we are tempted to be a diva inside of God's Kingdom. Tell the enemy to flee! You are here to accomplish the will of your Father. God wants to raise you up. He wants to give you honor and influence as long as your motive is to make His Name famous! There is nothing wrong with wanting to be successful. Just be sure it's His kind of success. Remember that children's church song, "This Little Light of Mine?" Honey, that said, "Hide it under a bushel: No! I'm gonna let it shine!" Religion says that fame is wrong, but God wants those who are sealed by His Name to tell the whole world!

The issue here is motive. What is your motive for wanting to be a well known minister? If your motive is rooted in humility, then great, but if it's fear based or pride based, then you are on the wrong path. I never began the ministry thinking "Ohhhh, I've got to be famous! I want a world-wide ministry and I want to be featured on TBN Cribs! I'll open my fridge and be like: Yeah! All that grape juice is for communion! What, what!" Obviously, there is no television show called "TBN Cribs" but you know what I'm saying. I've never aspired to be unknown either. I just sort of split the difference in my mind in the early years. But as the clarity of the calling on my life has grown, so have my dreams. There are things I believe the Lord wants me to share with the world. He will bless and enable me only as I am obedient and humble in His sight.

Maybe you are in Bible College reading this book. Maybe you went to Bible College to snag yourself a preacher husband. Let me fill you in on a little secret. The ministry is not a reality TV show. It is wonderful and honorable and

140

amazing...IF you're called. But even when you're called, it can be difficult and taxing. You can experience tremendous joy and excruciating pain. People will say they love you and then unapologetically spit in your face. They will criticize your children. They will condemn you every time you fail. They will use you and then leave you. Does that sound like the life of a celebrity? Remember how Jesus said that you'd receive a hundredfold in this life, but it would come with persecutions? That's what I'm talking about. You will never have a church full of people who are perfect. It's a fact. The reason your husband has a job is because of imperfect people. But when you have a servant's heart, and not a diva attitude, you are fulfilled by pouring your life into those around you.

Humility and servanthood do not mean that you are a door mat! Jesus is not asking you to lie down and be walked all over. Jesus was boldness clothed in humility! He faced the religious crowd with words like "snakes and vipers". He told them their father was the devil! He walked into the Temple, turned over tables and sent the money changers running. He declared the truth! He had righteous anger and He acted on it without sinning. Jesus is a living example of strength without pride! He was clothed in humility and still had multitudes following Him.

How to Never Fall Prey to the "Diva Syndrome"

1. Never, ever, ever believe the lie that you will get to a place in your ministry where you do not need a spiritual authority.

Have you ever been on a long flight and when you landed thought, "yes, we're here!" Only to discover that you were only stopping for a lay-over in some random city? It's so disappointing. The Holy Spirit said to me one day "When you think you have 'arrived' at your destination, you'll quickly find that you're simply experiencing a pride lay-over." He was reminding me that I better check myself before I wreck myself! You don't "arrive" in the Kingdom until you get to Heaven. You are to continually grow in all areas of your life.

2. Know the difference in accountability partners and secret keepers.

As I've studied the failures of different ministries I have come to realize that they have one common thread. Instead of surrounding themselves with authority and accountability they created a fortress of secret keepers. Here is the difference:

- Accountability partners are trustworthy confidants. Secret keepers are enablers. Accountability partners love you for who you are. Love covers a multitude of sin. It forgives (1 Peter 4:8).

- Accountability partners see you as an investment. Secret keepers see you as a commodity. Secret keepers need you for your position. Pride covers up a multitude of sin. It conceals (Proverbs 16:17-19; 2 Samuel 11 & 12; David, Bathsheba, & Nathan the Prophet).

3. Humble leadership is being an influencer, not a diva dictator.

Leadership is not defined completely by position. You can be the boss and still have none of your employees respect you or follow your direction. You can be a dictator and everyone rebel against you. The old statement is true: "You're not a leader unless you have followers. Otherwise, you're simply taking a walk."

4. Humble leadership will bring Godly promotion and Godly promotion will bring more responsibility.

Honor and entitlement are two different things. The Lord wants to honor the humble. But we have too many people walking around feeling entitled to everything from an entourage to free television time because they felt the tingle of the anointing once and three people fell out when they touched them. Psalm 147:6 states, "The Lord lifts up the humble; He casts the wicked to the ground." Proverbs 18:12 and 16 remind us, "Before destruction the heart of a man is haughty, and before honor is humility...A man's gift makes room for him and brings him before great men."

5. Humble leadership requires sacrifice and hard work.

First Timothy 2:15 tells us, "Be diligent to present yourself approved to God, a worker who does not need to be ashamed, rightly dividing the Word of truth." Go after your dreams with all your heart. Never let a spirit of intimidation disguise itself as humility and speak into your life! God created you to fly. His ways are higher than our ways! His thoughts are higher than our thoughts! Stay away from pompous roosters and prideful peacocks. They strut around looking for attention because they know they really can't get too far. Dare to soar with the eagles. When you let the Lord be your strength and the Holy Spirit be the wind of your empowerment, you'll quickly find the sky is the limit!

Chapter 8

40 Rules to Live By Everyday

1. Take a nap on Sunday if at all possible.

2. Keep your house and car clean.

3. Make your children behave.

4. Be involved in the worship service, especially during the altar time whether through singing or praying.

5. Ask the Lord to baptize you in the Holy Spirit with the evidence of speaking in a heavenly language and then pray in the Spirit daily.

6. Ask God for supernatural occurrences to be normal in your life and ministry.

7. Attend church every service unless there is an emergency.

8. "Amen" your husband. People will notice your support.

9. Stay out of credit card debt.

10. Don't brag.

11. Don't lie.

12. Don't choose sides between church people, especially not publicly.

13. Be friendly and smile.

14. Take pride in your appearance.

15. Don't say everything that comes to your mind…especially at women's meetings.

16. Don't take things personally.

17. Don't apologize for the Blessing on your life.

18. Don't apologize for the Favor of God on your life.

19. Give God ALL the Glory for everything good in your life.

20. Be sensitive to other minister's circumstances, when you're excited about yours.

21. Be early to church – never late.

22. Attend ministerial events and conferences with your husband as often as possible.

23. Don't nag your husband or children.

24. Don't be an emotional manipulator.

25. Don't be a snob.

26. Don't be a diva.

27. Don't sing if you stink at it.

28. Don't be a control freak.

29. Watch out for "Jezebel". She wants your husband, your ministry, and your life.

30. Exercise regularly.

31. Spend time alone with God everyday.

32. Don't feel obligated to let everyone hold your baby.

33. Stay in the Word through study, podcasts, books, CD's, DVD's, and Christian television.

34. Never do anything that you would undo if you got caught.

35. You're not responsible for how others act. You're only responsible for how you react.

36. Discuss spiritual things with your husband often. Keep one another challenged.

37. Discuss non-spiritual things with your husband often. Keep one another laughing.

38. Cry in God's presence.

39. Laugh at yourself.

40. Laugh at every enemy – God is on your side.

Wedding program

Our beautiful girls 2012

Our Family February 2013

Adjusting Mark's mic on our first Sunday in Atlanta, GA

Our original staff at The Tab

Our predecessors and friends, Sam & Jeanne Mayo

Altar service

Praise and worship at The Tab

Board members praying over Mark to begin the New Year

Our daughter, Julie, in ministry

Panama 2008

Panama 2008

Where we meet God every Sunday

My beautiful mother, sisters, and me

Mom and her precious husband, Chuck

My maternal grandparents, Rev Albert and Martha Davis: Over 50 years of pastoral ministry

My daddy and me

Dad and his sweet wife, Lisa

Mark's sister, Amy and her husband, Joel, and son, Landon

My amazing in laws: Rev CL and Aileen Haston

Mark and Riley

Julie and me ministering together

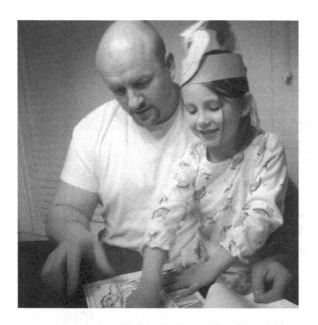

Mark spending time with Mackenzie before he left for East Africa

Real Estate days

Us with Pastor John Hagee, Pastor Happy Caldwell and an Israeli Representative

Mark and me with our spiritual covering, Pastor Ron Phillips

Us with Paul Crouch, founder and president of Trinity Broadcasting Network

Child dedication service

Mark and me...on top of the world

About the author:

Cheree' Haston is a third generation pastor's wife with a great spirit filled heritage that has become her life's foundation. She is full of stories and examples from her own experiences that will keep you laughing while challenging you to go deeper with the Lord!

Cheree' has been writing music and works of literature since she was a twelve year old girl. She is an anointed worship leader and travels several times a year to lead at conferences as well as weekly at her home church.

But Cheree's passion is to see the body of Christ grow through practical teaching and experiences with the Lord and one another. She and her husband, Mark, are especially drawn to helping other ministers fulfill their destiny!

Mark and Cheree' have been married and in full time ministry for nearly 20 years. They have three beautiful daughters, Julie, Riley, and Mackenzie and currently reside in Atlanta, GA where they pastor a beautiful group of international believers at The Tabernacle.